REDMOND O'HANLON is best known for his journeys into some of the most remote jungles of the world. His books include *Congo Journey, Into the Heart of Borneo, In Trouble Again* and *Trawler.*

RUDI ROTTHIER is a Flemish journalist and author. In 2004 he won the Bob den Uyl book prize for travel writing for *The Qur'an Route.*

THE FETISH ROOM

THE FETISH ROOM

The Education of a Naturalist

REDMOND O'HANLON
&
RUDI ROTTHIER

Translated by Jane Hedley-Prôle

P

PROFILE BOOKS

First published in Great Britain in 2011 by
PROFILE BOOKS LTD
3a Exmouth House
Pine Street
London EC1R 0JH
www.profilebooks.com

First published in the Netherlands by Atlas entitled
God, Darwin en natuur

Copyright © Rudi Rotthier and Redmond O'Hanlon, 2009, 2011
Translation copyright © Jane Hedley-Prôle, 2011

1 3 5 7 9 10 8 6 4 2

Typeset in Quadraat by MacGuru Ltd
info@macguru.org.uk
Printed and bound in Great Britain by
Clays, Bungay, Suffolk

A CIP catalogue record for this book is available from the British Library.

ISBN 978 1 84668 414 2
eISBN 978 1 84765 452 6

The paper this book is printed on is certified by the © 1996 Forest Stewardship
Council A.C. (FSC). It is ancient-forest friendly. The printer holds FSC chain of
custody SGS-COC-2061

FSC
Mixed Sources
Product group from well-managed
forests and other controlled sources
Cert no. SGS-COC-2061
www.fsc.org
© 1996 Forest Stewardship Council

CONTENTS

The photographs in this book are by Emile Brugman, except that on p. 54 which is from Redmond O'Hanlon's collection

Chapter 1

INTRODUCTION TO CHAOS

Redmond is waiting on the other side of the railings, wearing a baggy blue shirt with a navy jumper knotted loosely round his neck. He waves enthusiastically, his arms flailing like windmills. We walk through the station to get to his side of the railings. His enthusiasm is undiminished; he launches into anecdotes, tells stories – mumbling rather – in fits and starts, hops from one subject to the next, hops back again, listens briefly, nods approval. 'Yes! But!' We get in the car and he drives away, confidently negotiating Oxford's fiendish one-way traffic system, his words even harder to make out against the background noise of traffic.

'I used to think a 30 mph speed limit was outrageous. These days 30 mph is too fast for me.' Frustrated younger drivers are apparently forever stuck behind him. 'Sometimes they're not even that young. Everyone gets stuck behind me.' He now believes himself to be the slowest driver in the universe. 'Arrggghh!'

Redmond O'Hanlon

But he has more pressing concerns to deal with. His wife Belinda has just had an operation and is being nursed in a private hospital that could take her at short notice, but that charges the astronomical fee of £2,000 a night. The same surgeon could have carried out the same procedure for free on the NHS if Belinda had been prepared to go on a waiting list and put up with the pain for a few months. Redmond doesn't know how long she will have to stay in hospital and how crippling the final bill will be. His anger at this two-tier system has by now abated somewhat.

Shouldn't he be with her?

He has been to see her, but she couldn't stand his hyperactivity for long and thought he ought to come to meet us.

Redmond fishes in his trouser pocket for his hearing aid. He turns out to have one for each ear, seemingly putting them in and taking them out at random. In the mornings his hearing is fine, he says, but as the day wears on it deteriorates. He sighs frequently. The extra weight that he carries makes him pant; even heaving the steering wheel round is an effort. He searches, sighing, for the five pence that will allow us to cross the toll bridge over the Thames. The bridge is unique. Privately owned, it is governed by its own act of parliament, which prohibits the construction of any other bridge across the Thames within a range of three miles up or downstream. Commuters want the toll to be abolished, they hate the delay it entails. Redmond seems rather to like the toll, to like things remaining as they are.

A lone man collects the toll in both directions. I try to calculate how many drivers are needed per hour to pay his salary. On this quiet Saturday evening there clearly isn't enough traffic for a decent wage.

Half an hour later, we arrive at Pelican House, Redmond's home in Church Hanborough.

We encounter a scene of chaos that can only partially be explained by his temporary bachelor status. Books overspill shelves or lie on the floor, layer upon layer. Pathways exist, but are sometimes blocked by piles of volumes, so that you have to take a bigger stride or hazard a leap to get from one spot to another. Tottering mounds of dirty crockery obscure the sink. Redmond has removed little piles of cat sick from view by the simple expedient of covering them with upturned, presumably clean, saucepans. He overfeeds his cats, he says, and this is the result. Standing a foot or so from such a pan, Redmond switches on the washing machine. It is a juxtaposition that I find pleasing. The act of laundering makes chaos habitable.

The toilet on the landing needs to be furnished with a bucket of water, pending a visit from the plumber, and the heating system appears to require insider knowledge and the application of matches. Whichever door you open, you see Redmond's books on display, along with photos of his travels and mementos. 'Here's my subconscious hanging on the wall,' he comments. I am given his son's room.

Redmond manages to find glasses somewhere and opens a bottle of bubbly.

But even though the operation casts something of a gloom, there is also good news. Plans are afoot to make a documentary about Redmond. He is to leave shortly for a six-month trip to Spitsbergen, home to some of the world's most abundant seabird colonies. His masterpiece, *Congo Journey*, has been reissued as a Penguin Classic. Most satisfying of all, perhaps, he has just learnt that a creature has been named after him. The letter telling him so is in a leather binder and therefore not too difficult to trace. 'Ha! Got it ... It's a childhood dream come true, you know. Of course, when I was small I fantasised about it being a huge great impressive beast.' He shows me what it has become in reality. The letter is from an entomologist in Los Angeles.

Dear M. O'Hanlon,

Please find enclosed a reprint of a paper I recently published in which I dedicate a new genus of clerid beetle to you. I hope you don't find this too presumptuous, and I assure you that in the scheme of things coleopteran, this is a very unusual and attractive critter, with no unsavoury habits.

I've enjoyed your writing for many years and I hope this patronymic goes some small way towards repaying you for the hours of pleasure your books have brought me. If you ever find yourself waylaid and bored in Los Angeles drop me a line and I will probably rustle up a cold beer and a hot curry.

Sincerely,
Jacques Rifkind

A photo is included of the beetle, the *Ohanlonella esperanzae Rifkind*, which is dark brown and 7.25 millimetres long. It was found in the Sierra de Juárez, Mexico, not so far from the border with North America. The official document in which the beetle is named states:

I take pleasure in naming this unusual new genus for the writer Redmond O'Hanlon, whose books have for many years inspired and entertained me with their rare combination of humor, insight and always impeccable natural history.

'I should make a copy of that,' Redmond muses aloud. The leather binder is put on a pile and instantly lost to sight under a pile of other things that he wants to show me. We slip out into his garden, scaling an artificial mound that overlooks a rolling landscape. The corn has been harvested; the stubble twinkles in the setting sun.

'How's your pond getting on?' I ask.

We have met on two earlier occasions. The first was in the early autumn of 2003, when I came to Pelican House for an interview following the publication of *Trawler*. Perhaps my memory is playing me tricks, but I don't recall the chaos being significantly less at the time. It may even be that things are exactly as they were. Items that I moved then might conceivably still be astray. We drank an awful lot of wine – the kind of consumption that one measures in bottles rather than glasses – Redmond more than anyone, but I much more than usual, which may explain why I remember so little.

But I have often thought back to a snippet of the conversation. Redmond, standing by the pond in his garden, claimed that you could tell from a man's reaction to the pond, or ponds in general, whether he had homosexual inclinations. According to his theory, men who didn't like gazing endlessly into ponds were gay. I like theories of this kind, because they are demonstrably indefensible and yet they have a certain appealing logic. They sound ridiculous, but are not. In the intervening five years I had been unable to pass a pond without gazing at it broodingly, bracing myself for a degree of self examination. Lakes, pools and ponds had forever lost their innocence as far as I was concerned.

We met again a few weeks later, in November 2003. He was visiting the Antwerp Book Fair and I was supposed to interview him. In the event I proved to be an unnecessary appendage, even an impediment (albeit a paid one), to the show that Redmond put on. If I remember correctly, he dismissed the first question with a wave of his arm, stood up and let loose a flood of stories, spiced up with pictures of sinister-looking fishes and preserved fish parts in jars. He enjoyed himself greatly, and so did his audience. Afterwards they went off and bought his books en masse.

The pond?

'It's got overgrown,' says Redmond, 'I should really clear it out.'

He potters around in the garden from time to time. The former explorer has turned gardener. He is considering enlarging his vegetable patch and raising his mound. At present it is only about a metre higher than the rest of the garden, but that metre makes a world of difference. At the base you are in your own world; at the top you enjoy a panorama. What might one not discover from the dizzy height of a metre and a half?

He opens another bottle and, as we sit at a corner of the table that has been freed from clutter, he talks about his changing views on life.

'When I was young I pictured being old along the following lines. You would walk with a stick but still be in full possession of your mental powers. The same would apply to your friends. You would drink the odd glass of wine and say "Do you remember when ...?" My assumption was that everyone would be able to recall the occasion in question and take pleasure in these memories. Nowadays I perceive such contacts with old friends as less essential. It's not that having a cat is sufficient, but ...'

Redmond does a final spot of gardening and then departs, sighing, with Bertie the cat, in the direction of bed.

His repeated references to degeneration and age, possibly

prompted by Belinda's operation, begin to perturb me. He was born in 1947, which makes him sixty-one.

'It's a good age', he says suddenly. 'You still accomplish the odd thing, but people no longer expect very much of you.' This remark, too, is disarming rather than cheerful.

Fortunately, I am not the only visitor, so I can linger in the background occasionally and observe Redmond interacting with my two companions: Emile Brugman, director of the Atlas publishing company, who came up with the idea of a joint book, and Ellen Schalker, his partner, also an old Atlas stalwart. The three have known each other since the early 1980s, when Redmond's first book, Into the Heart of Borneo, was published. They share anecdotes and acquaintances. There is a lot of catching up to do. Redmond is keen to know who Emile thinks should get this year's Nobel Prize for literature.

Redmond occupies an uneasy space in his own house. As he walks past the sink full of dirty crockery he looks a little bemused, as if wondering whether the pile might disappear spontaneously. When his guests take it upon themselves to remove items from it and wash them, he is not at all put out.

Our host has been shopping, so we are well provisioned for breakfast the next morning. An abundance of sausages, bacon and eggs confronts us; we manage to make some inroads, at least on the bread. A steady supply of milk is delivered to the door. The fridge is full of bottles, half open, half untouched.

After breakfast we drive to the market town of Abingdon, to see an exhibition featuring Belinda's life's work: Annabelinda couture design. We take Belinda's car as the roomier of the two, the back seat of Redmond's having disappeared under piles of documents and general detritus.

Abingdon dates from Roman times and once possessed a fine Saxon abbey, which fell into ruin after Henry VIII dissolved the monasteries. A large gaol, built by prisoners of the Napoleonic Wars, still survives. Much else has been destroyed, as the town was heavily bombed in the Second World War. Its pleasant historic centre is surrounded by a hotchpotch of postwar architecture; concrete structures clash with traditional-style buildings.

Trying to squeeze Belinda's car into what later turns out to be a closed car park, Redmond bumps into a concrete post. Although the impact is only slight, the damage is spectacular: the back windscreen shatters with a bang. It is hard to know why; it didn't even seem to come into contact with the post. Ellen fumbles for something in her handbag. When Redmond notices this, he comes up with a theory that, at times of shock or crisis, women rearrange their handbags. In fact Ellen wasn't rearranging anything, but that doesn't disprove the theory. Redmond subsequently manages to find a secure car park where the vehicle can be left in relative safety, even without a rear windscreen.

The exhibition is housed in the old town hall, an angular, seventeenth-century building. The clothes on show – all designed, produced and sold by Belinda – are strikingly unconventional, a cross between hippy outfits and mediaeval robes: perhaps tending more towards the mediaeval than the hippy. Well-crafted, made of solid materials in soft, timeless tints, they would not look out of place on a Pre-Raphaelite canvas. When you spread out a ball gown it is as if you are unfolding a tapestry.

Benazir Bhutto wore clothes from Annabelinda when she was at Oxford.

Unknown to Belinda, the notorious drug dealer Howard Marks, better known as 'Mr Nice', was running his criminal empire from a floor of the building in which Annabelinda was housed. Marks, who had previously been married to one of Belinda's friends, had suggested to Belinda and her business partner Anita that they move from their previous premises to this larger building. The two women were blissfully unaware that Annabelinda had thus become a respectable front for his illegal activities. Belinda simply thought of him as someone who spent his days stoned in bed with his second wife.

Other hippy memories surface. One day a traveller returned from Afghanistan, with a rucksack of antique Chinese braids. Belinda offered him ninety pounds for the lot, promptly incorporating the finds in her designs.

Redmond tells me that Belinda has always paid herself less than her highest paid employee. Back in the 1970s it was something of a credo that everyone should be treated equally and that managers should be content with a modest salary. 'But unlike other people, she's always remained true to that principle.'

The exhibition came about following Belinda's decision to sell the business, which she had run since 1971 – her friend Anita having moved on long ago in search of other horizons – and enjoy her retirement.

Some of Annabelinda's old publicity material hangs between the gowns and wedding dresses.

To pleasure your potentate: pure silk pyjamas from Annabelinda.

To turtle dove all summer: spring plumage from Annabelinda.

William Harvey of Oxford: discoverer of the circulation of the blood. Annabelinda of Oxford: discoverer of ways to make it circulate a little faster.

Don't be Freudened, release his repressions in an Annabelinda nightdress.

For the greater delight of your paramour, Annabelinda will make you a pinafore.

Annabelinda, dress designers of genius: for formal receptions into Royal Societies, for clandestine meetings in unmentionable places; for gala performances at the opera (and at later hours elsewhere); for the nuptials of Princesses of the Blood Royal; for the greater pleasure of discerning voyeurs at major events of the sporting calendar; for ducal invitations to discreet hunting lodges lost in ancestral forests, order your carriage to Annabelinda.

Who thought up all this copy? Redmond smiles discreetly. Apparently he wrote the ads at night, or during days at Annabelinda when he was working on his PhD. Belinda put them in the *Daily Information*, Oxford's student paper, *Vogue* and the *Observer*. Redmond's first earnings as a writer came from these one-liners and advertisements.

The clientele was as eccentric as the publicity. Initially consisting of students whose grants were burning a hole in their pockets, it was later made up of academics and the well-to-do, aristocratic ladies who wanted something a bit daring. At first, clothes were made on demand, and were tailored to individual requirements. Later, Annabelinda produced collections, mainly for parties and weddings, targeting the upper end of the market.

We drive on to Oxford, where Redmond wants to visit Belinda. To everyone's surprise, she is discharged from the hospital there and then, which necessitates some on-the-spot planning. Still heavily medicated, one minute she is bright and alert, the next she loses the thread and dozes off. But she is pleased I am there, and starts to make all kinds of plans. She wants to ring the insurance company, and get someone to repair her car.

'What will you two be doing?' she asks.

Our answer takes too long in coming. In fact, we don't yet have an answer. Belinda falls asleep.

In general, I don't much like planning. In general, I am well-disposed towards chaos. Vague suggestions have been made, things that, by definition, can only be vague. A joint book. A book about Darwin, about perceptions of nature, about God.

By anyone's lights, we two are as different as chalk and cheese. I am hard put to tell a great tit from a robin, whereas Redmond can identify the bird that woke him up just by its song. He is a traveller; he looks for animals in remote places. He wants to discover things, to be the first. In that sense he is an explorer, whereas I, even in remote places, am above all a people-watcher. People fascinate me, even when they have abandoned their original traditions and been run over by the steamroller of colonial civilisation. I distrust originality. He tends to travel in company, I prefer to journey alone. He complains endlessly about his poor physical condition, whereas I am training for a marathon. We have both turned our backs on religion, though his case is somewhat more dramatic than mine, his father being a vicar. Perhaps the greatest difference between us is that he is a dramatic figure, with his wild hair and side whiskers, his sweeping gestures and loud laugh. I prefer to blend into the landscape, figuratively speaking. As far as I am concerned, nature is optional. If all the descriptions of nature were to be scrapped from my books, only about five pages would be lost.

We share a disease, cerebral malaria, which could have killed us both.

In preparation – for what? – I have read and re-read Darwin's works, an enjoyable task. I am familiar with Redmond's books, having read them when they came out. I have deliberately avoided reading interviews with him, or articles about him. What can we talk about? He is an expert in fields I know nothing about, and for obvious reasons he knows next to nothing about me. Perhaps he has a trapped brainchild, and I will become the midwife of a book he hasn't been able to write. Perhaps it will all come to nothing. It is too soon to start worrying about things, though.

The visitors disappear for the night, to stay at the King's Arms in Woodstock and let Redmond and Belinda catch their breath.

The next day Belinda is able to stay alert for longer periods. Neither she nor the rescue party of children, consisting of daughter Puffin and her younger brother Galen, are inclined to entrust Redmond with the care of an invalid. The children are going to take their mother to the farm in Kent that she inherited from her parents. However advanced the surgery, she has undergone a major operation and will need many weeks to recover. The children have taken over the reins and are preparing a meal.

The house is licked into shape before our eyes. The mess is cleared away without impacting on the chaos. The cat sick is swept up. 'We love our father,' said Puffin, 'but he's not exactly a New Man.'

Redmond's wife Belinda

It turns out that I blundered by leaving the door of Galen's room open, therefore making it accessible to cats. One of the cats spent the night with me. Galen is allergic to cats. The episode revives a long-running argument between Redmond and Belinda. Redmond feels that Galen is making an unnecessary fuss. Belinda fears that Galen will no longer visit them if his room makes him sneeze.

But the cooking proceeds in high spirits. And Emile, Redmond and I are left alone in what I shall call the dining room, the room that somewhere contains the leather binder with the beetle that was named after Redmond, and is home to the Penguin edition of *Congo Journey*.

Redmond starts to tell stories, which I tape. When he talks, he is transformed. He concentrates, builds up to a punchline and gesticulates to fill gaps or pauses when he is racking his memory. He leaps up, looks for documentary evidence, then sits down again, entertaining himself as much as his listeners. He groans, either in a personal capacity or on behalf of the people in one of his stories. Little cries escape his lips. He still hops from one subject to another – an incorrigible trait, according to Belinda. Stories flow, not necessarily chronologically, one memory sparks another and Redmond more often than not fails to make the link clear. But the stories are, like their narrator, dramatic, and a book suddenly becomes less hypothetical. He will recount and I will record: that seems like a fair arrangement.

'There was a boy called Crane in my class at secondary school who dreamt of becoming a surgeon. Once we were dissecting a frog or a rat in our biology class and the teacher saw that he had cut through the animal's spinal cord. He said, "But Crane, you might just as well have cut off its head." So Crane abandoned his ambition of becoming a surgeon. Instead he became a GP and married a nurse. I ran across him recently, and it turned out his practice wasn't far from here, on the other side of Abingdon.

Prior to that he'd practised in the Outer Hebrides. He made it a point of honour always to tell the truth, no matter what the circumstances were. For instance, if he was called to assist at a delivery late in the evening he would say, "I'm fairly drunk, but I'll do my very best." After a while he had to leave. He came to the conclusion that he needed a niche in which he could flourish. He opted for hypnosis, got a job in a hospital and started to hypnotise patients. You know the kind of thing, "Picture to yourself that you're walking beside a beautiful river. Everything's very peaceful; you can feel your heartbeat slowing down ..." And it worked! His patients fell asleep on command. But according to Crane, "The problem was that I was such a good hypnotist I invariably hypnotised myself into the bargain." One morning the cleaning shift entered his room to find both doctor and patient fast asleep in their chairs. "My bottom was incredibly sore", Crane said. I asked, "What about the patient?" "Oh, his was pretty sore, too." Apart from the sore bottom, he appeared not to think that there was anything remarkable about what had happened. He told the story with a perfectly innocent candour. But of course he didn't keep that job very long either.'

Before we know it, we are once again plunged into one of Redmond's crazy theories. Proposition: the First World War is the fault of Christianity; more precisely, of Protestant boarding schools.

'In 1851 the Great Exhibition was held in Crystal Palace to celebrate modern industrial technology and design. Britain was at the height of its power, and led the way in scientific advances. But which country, twenty years later, was to set up schools with superb science departments? Germany. They dropped Latin, while British schools hung on to the classical curriculum. The Germans kicked out the clergymen and the classics, and trained boys to become engineers and scientists. The First World War might not have happened if British schools had undergone a similar transformation. At the time Britain was such an invincible naval power that it feared no attack, but its might soon ebbed away. It's true that the Germans used to say "Gott mit uns" (to which our troops would reply, "We've got mittens too"), but they learnt how to build machines at those schools before they picked up a bible. If we'd done likewise, if we'd booted the clergymen out of our schools and banished Latin, there would never have been an arms race and we wouldn't have had a war.'

So the British Empire was destroyed by the clergy? 'Absolutely. Clergymen and the classics. Take Josiah Wedgwood, John Dalton, James Watt and George Stephenson, for instance. Some of the finest minds in the country. What did they do with their sons? They sent them to schools where their heads were stuffed with Latin and Greek. Did they think this would equip them to take over the family business or make scientific discoveries?'

Emile points out that the grandson of one of these fine minds, Erasmus Darwin, sailed on the Beagle and formulated the theory of evolution. 'Yes,' counters Redmond, 'but he very nearly became a parish priest instead. And people looked down on you if you went into business, because they rated knowledge of a dead language much more highly.'

It is time for dinner. Afterwards Belinda and the children depart for Kent.

After those initial conversations Redmond suggests that we shift headquarters to The Bell, his local, for a couple of days. Belinda does not really approve of it, but she is no longer here. He proposes that we sit on the terrace, overlooking Blenheim Palace and its two thousand acres of parkland, order pints of Old Tripp – the local brew – and talk.

He anticipates this with particular delight, because on a recent visit to the hostelry in question, the pub dog dashed across his table for a romp in a neighbouring meadow. He is firmly convinced that the dog will perform the same manoeuvre on the stroke of five. That is something to look forward to, a hilarious moment when the pint glasses will wobble precariously as the dog vaults between them.

Hey, I think: that's something we have in common. A longing for the hilarious. For the fixed order and expectations to be disrupted. Though what do I mean by fixed order, actually?

And what will we talk about?

'No idea. We'll think of something. Emile thinks we'll think of something. He was talking about a new genre. Part biography, part nature writing, part Darwin. How difficult can that be?'

Redmond drives us to Oxford, where Emile and Ellen are to take the train back. Ellen and I clamber into the rear passenger seat of his car, inserting ourselves between piles of rubbish and what are undoubtedly important documents.

He suddenly hears a siren.

'I've always regarded ambulances with awe and amazement. When I was a student they didn't yet have sirens. Even then I thought, how wonderful that people need your expertise so urgently. That will never happen to me: people wanting to know something about Milton so badly that the traffic has to be disrupted. I wish it were otherwise.'

He needs that sense of urgency, he says. Drama and pain. You need drama and pain to write. What other possible subject is there?

'When Annabelinda was starting up I used to drive into Oxford with Belinda in the early morning. I'm not a morning person, but no matter how bad I felt, I would go with her in her van. I would then walk to the Bodleian Library, that wonderful building, with its eight or nine million books. I was almost always the first there, but sometimes I was pipped at the post by an Indian PhD student. The reading room boasted only a single armchair. That was my goal, my point of focus. If the Indian student had managed to occupy it first, my whole day was ruined. Eventually, night owl though I was, I encouraged Belinda to leave even earlier, for fear that the bastard would pinch my chair. He was no doubt equally fed up when I grabbed it. If I was victorious, I would sit in that chair all day, looking out of the window, reading, enjoying the silence and my surroundings, the ancient architecture. The focus of the whole town is on appreciating intellect and books above all else. You tread pavement that was trodden in earlier times by the feet of people who were sunk in thought, who were turning over new ideas and pondering the state of the world, or the state of their field of expertise. It's quite a shock to realise that there are places where people never voluntarily pick up a book. In the rarefied air of Oxford you would never suspect that such Philistinism existed. I could have spent the rest of my life in that chair in the Bodleian.'

Things turned out differently. Everything turned out differently.

That evening, in The Bell, armed with impressive glasses of Old Tripp, he seems relieved. Belinda has weathered the operation well. The children have assumed care of her, rescuing her from domestic chaos and their father's incompetence. 'I wouldn't have minded looking after her myself. I would have done so gladly, but no one seems to think that I could. I think I could.'

The last few days have gone well. The insurance company will pay for the rear windscreen to be replaced. A plumber is coming to look at the toilet on the landing.

Why don't we go on a journey together, he asks. 'What could be more natural than two travel writers travelling together? At least, if you trust me to drive. Let's draw up a list. You write it.'

What kind of list?

'Things we have to do tomorrow.'

Like?

'The stone circles at Avebury, you have to see those. There's a hotel nearby that I've always wanted to stay at. And Marlborough, my old school. My father's vicarage in Calne. We can easily do all that.'

By the time we get back from the pub to Pelican House he has already expanded his travel plans. The Dorset coast, his birthplace and his primary school are now also on the programme.

And Darwin's house in Kent, I suggest.

Of course, and perhaps Belinda's farm. And Salisbury Cathedral, whose spire the RAF used for target practice during the Second World War. Redmond's mind is seething with plans.

'And we'll get up early tomorrow. Let's say at nine o'clock.'

I move from his son's room to his daughter's room, where the window may be opened and cats are allowed. The thought occurs to me that when I wake up tomorrow I still won't know which bird is singing.

Chapter 2

BACK TO THE VICARAGE

Two travel writers in a blue Clio. What, indeed, could be more natural? The sky is a lighter blue, the leaves are turning brown. The sight of Redmond – full of energy and obviously in high spirits – fills me with confidence. He has brought along hiking boots for me, because we might encounter some mud. He offers me a caffeine pill.

Who needs caffeine pills after drinking coffee?

'It helps me keep my energy levels up.'

Redmond drives and I keep a vague eye on our route. This is necessary, he explains, because for some reason or other he can't navigate, could never navigate, from Pelican House to his parental home in Calne. Something prevents him. Some strange unknown cause makes him lose his way.

'I always had my doubts about Freud, but ...'

Redmond often uses the word 'but'. 'But' truncates his thoughts. It bursts out of his mouth with a pop, followed by a pause. 'But' signals a change of course.

'Can you add an item to the list? We need stamps.'

This morning, in addition to the milk, some urgent letters have arrived for Belinda at Pelican House and he wants to send them on to Kent. The stamps are added to the list, along with petrol, which we will need fairly soon. Along with a roll of film in case he wants to take photos of the vicarage, which he is keen to show me.

Signposts are sadly lacking in these rural areas. We have only proceeded about seven miles from Pelican House before Redmond takes a wrong turning. He immediately realises his mistake, slams on the brakes and turns the car round. His co-pilot issues instructions at the next turning.

'Freud again.'

So, the explorer has no sense of direction?

'I can't read maps either. These days, expeditions rely on GPS. No wonder they come back so soon. I was always lost for several weeks at least.'

What makes Calne such a difficult destination?

'How much time have you got?'

We have time in abundance, surely?

'I suppose we have. Anyway, a few years ago I was seeing doctors and therapists and someone asked me what went through my mind when I contemplated the death of my mother, who was still alive at the time. I said, "I know where I can rent a .45 Magnum and I would buy two magazines of bullets. I would stand at her grave, holding the gun with both hands – because it's quite heavy – and empty the two magazines into the grave to make sure that she had really snuffed it." I thought that was funny, but nobody laughed.'

That doesn't surprise me.

'It doesn't surprise me now, either. But at the time it did. Instead of laughing, someone started feverishly taking notes.'

The first stop on our itinerary is Marlborough, the little town where Redmond went to secondary school. A memory surfaces of getting into trouble. One day he found a skull in the cemetery and, in the spirit of Byron, decided to use it as a drinking vessel for a mind-expanding brew. He was caught, but not expelled, because the literary allusion gave panache to his vandalism.

How did it taste?

'Not as special as I'd hoped.'

That is one of his relatively pleasant memories.

When he thinks back to the masters, Redmond shudders ostentatiously.

'Terrible men.' It was they who caned the boys. 'In those days, the teachers wore loose, grey flannel trousers. We thought they always got an erection when they caned you. That's why they became teachers. They felt your bottom beforehand to make sure you hadn't stuffed newspapers down your trousers. Still, that was better than prep school, where you first had to take off your pyjama bottoms.

Corporal punishment was part of the education system. We were told that we were being moulded to help administer the greatest empire the world had ever known. The walls were hung with portraits of former pupils, who had become bishops or generals. I was there in the early 1960s. Someone should have told them that there was very little left of that empire.

Marlborough College was founded in the mid-nineteenth century to educate the sons of Church of England clergy. Compared to a truly prestigious school like Winchester, which dates back to the Middle Ages, or Eton, it was a rather second-rate establishment. As the son of a clergyman I was one of the poor boys, so my fees were halved. Youths from moneyed families had private rooms with staff; I slept in a dormitory with thirteen other boys. At night the housemaster would creep through the dorms to check we weren't masturbating.

We didn't have any chairs and the lavatories had no doors, because you could commit sodomy behind a door: sodomy seemed to be very much on the masters' minds. As a new boy, aged about thirteen, you had to stand next to your bed in the nude and sing a song. Every morning you walked from the dormitory to the bathroom. On the first morning the older boys stood in the corridor, armed with wet towels and flicked you as you went past. Then you were …'

One of them?

'Yes.'

His face takes on a serious expression.

'But. The laboratories were excellent. Much better than in other schools. Instead of studying in the library, I would sneak over to the biology laboratory, where I could peer through the microscope and discover magical things. I would slip out down the fire escape, feeling that I was being naughty. That helped preserve my interest in biology. It seemed like stolen pleasure.'

Were there any masters you liked?

'Oh yes. Quite a few actually. Including some I've remained grateful to ever since. The English teacher was one. And the wonderful biology teacher, Jack Halliday, who was immensely fat and hairy. I hung on his every word from lesson one.' He imitates a low, steely voice, "Good morning boys. We are going to learn about biology. 'Bio' means life, 'ology' means study. It will involve an awful lot of sex and I will tell you all about it." He drew beautiful diagrams. As he drew, he became completely immersed in what he was doing and would forget that we were there; his left hand would gradually disappear into his trousers and he would start to scratch his bum. I thought, what a man! When he taught us about kidneys he brought one with him to the class. He flourished the bloody object in the air and announced, "I'm going to eat this for lunch." Arrgghh!'

Redmond had intended to break the journey in Hungerford, but the traffic system has changed and a host of one-way streets have sprung up to trap us. For a while we follow road signs that promise to take us to 'all destinations', but we never manage to get to where Redmond wants to be. So we turn round, rejoin the main road and leave Hungerford and its undoubtedly unforgettable attractions behind.

About six miles further on, just outside Marlborough, Redmond takes the turning for Savernake Forest. The forest is privately owned but publicly accessible. It is ancient: the name can be found in chronicles going back to the tenth century. John Seymour owned the forest when Henry VIII hunted there and his daughter Jane briefly became one of the King's wives. Today the place is deserted, and the beech trees are the realm of the birds. 'Lots of jays,' Redmond remarks. 'It's a great place for birdsong ... I used to come here on the bike when school got too much for me.'

A place to forget the misery of everyday life?

'Yes. I could escape in the natural world and my cares would vanish. I've always been fortunate in being able to do that. Just like the biology lab; there was so much to discover here that I didn't have time to feel miserable.'

It is market day in Marlborough, which makes parking difficult.

We are to have a kidney-free lunch in the bowels of a pub called The Dungeon. He orders cottage pie, while I opt for bangers and mash: a favourite dish at Redmond's school, apparently, and a staple meal of his youth. My order comes with peas and lashings of dark gravy. The contents of his pie are more difficult to identify, though meat appears to be a component. 'Junk that it's better not to enquire about. Mmmm.'

Redmond pops another caffeine pill.

He takes other pills too, he tells me, antidepressants. 'Otherwise I'd fall apart.'

Yet he makes a cheerful impression.

'I do now, but there are days when nothing can interest me. I can't even bring myself to write a letter or a card. Everything seems insurmountable. It is insurmountably hard to sit still and yet insurmountably hard to get out of one's chair. At times like those the pills help. Stephen Fry made a brilliant, extremely courageous television series about manic depression and depression in general. Belinda and I watched it together. I sat there nodding away, happily convinced that none of it applied to me. Belinda didn't say anything, but I could see from her expression that she thought differently about the matter ...

You asked just now why it isn't easy to find the way to Calne. In order to be able to write, I've always felt that I had to somehow convince myself that I never had parents. I needed to erase their images and presence, otherwise I wouldn't have been able to write a single sentence. They despised literature; in fact they regarded books – at least the books that I value – as vile, indecent, an absurd waste of time. I banished them from my thoughts for thirty years.

But when you get into your late fifties that doesn't work any more. For some reason or other you don't have enough energy to fight your past. It bursts through a kind of dam and threatens to drown you. I found I lacked the drive and devotion to work every evening from eight or nine until two or three in the morning. That had always been my method, because when darkness falls, books come to life for me. The family suffers, of course. When I write I feel permanently oppressed. I live

Bertie the cat

in my own little world; I'm not open to domestic life ... Now that I have stopped writing I am on an even keel and the cat loves me.' A guffaw makes people at other tables jump. 'Bertie always loves me.'

Has the urge to travel deserted you, too?

'Absolutely. Spitsbergen has its appeal of course. I'll get to see a lot of birds – not birds that are unknown to me, but in greater numbers than I've ever seen before – and the biology of the northern seas is enthralling. When I was researching *Trawler*, I never expected to be captivated by fish, but marine life and its evolution are truly fascinating. The problem with Spitsbergen is that the only people who live there are scientists and miners. It has never had a local community. It won't be an unpleasant experience, I can put up with hardship and I'm still interested, but ...

Some time ago I spent a year on Orkney. In theory I could write about that, but something prevents me. I think the problem is that it didn't entail enough suffering. Now there's a truly Protestant notion: you must suffer to earn your book.

God blesses only those who suffer. That's been a leitmotif for much of my life. You have to let yourself be beaten to a pulp on the rugby field to earn approval. If you're struck down by malaria or hepatitis and put your life at risk, you must be a real man. That's how the Protestant ethic works: if someone is not suffering, there's something wrong with them. They're decadent, they're not blessed by God.

Writing a book is of course also a form of deferred pleasure. You start one knowing that it will take ages to finish. Perhaps as long as ten years. At my age ...'

You don't think that time is on your side anymore.

'That's it.'

At your age, Norman Lewis was only just getting up to speed.

'He's my hero. He wrote his best work when he was over seventy-three, according to his biographer. So perhaps there's hope after all. Perhaps there is hope after Rudi ...'

There is no one left to be startled by another guffaw: the Dungeon has emptied.

It seems that Redmond has two ways of stressing points or putting them in perspective. His guffaw, which is infectious and loud but never quite loud enough to bury tragedy under hilarity, and an expression of horror, accompanied by a cry of 'Arrggghh' and a lot of hand waving. So far, his 'Arrggghh' is more innocent than his guffaw.

He leads me to the other side of the market square, to the White Horse Bookshop.

'This is where I used my prize money to buy my first Penguin Classics.'

And now he is himself a Penguin Classic.

'I am indeed!'

One of his schoolboy purchases was Darwin's *Origin of Species*.

The shop does not have it in stock at the moment. Redmond doesn't give me time to find out whether they do have *Congo Journey*. The place is under different management now. There used to be special shelves for Penguins, but these have made way for displays of colouring pencils and book jackets.

Redmond recalls reading his Darwin Penguin Classic in bed by the light of a torch. It was a revelation that almost instantly liberated him from God.

'Belinda went to a Catholic school run by nuns. The nuns tried to convince her that she had a vocation. She was called to the mother superior, who was considered to be virtually a saint. Not only was she credited with feats of levitation – it being alleged that she occasionally hovered a few feet above her bed – she was also thought to fast permanently. But one day she was careless and left traces of egg around her mouth, which cast doubts on her holiness and permanent fasting, and possibly even on her feats of levitation. Anyway, she tried to persuade Belinda to join the order. Belinda had a pony, called Kismet, and she asked, 'Will Kismet be with me in heaven?' The mother superior said categorically, 'No, there are no animals in heaven.' Belinda became an atheist on the spot. She must have been about sixteen. It was the opposite of a Pauline conversion; a lightning de-Christianisation.

In my case it was Darwin who settled it. Many butterflies have eye-like patterns on their wings. They are very beautiful, as my father would say. They were put there by God, he would go on to say, in order to make us glad. What, by contrast, does Darwin tell us? The sparrow advances on the butterfly. The butterfly flaps its wings open, and two large eyes suddenly appear. The sparrow sees an owl's eyes, wets itself, and falls out of the hedge. The butterfly flaps away unharmed.'

Truly Darwinian language, I remark, sparrows wetting themselves.

'Absolutely. If the choice is between the Good Lord decorating the butterfly's wings with lovely eye patterns, and the butterfly developing an eye pattern as the result of natural selection, there's no real competition is there? Darwin is so much better. That image of the butterfly confusing the sparrow was what convinced me.

My father always used to say, our lives are hard, but God has surrounded us with exquisite creatures to console us. The gorgeous plumage of birds, the graceful beauty of deer – that kind of thing. As some of his books on natural theology put it: there will always be nettles, but God in His goodness has put dock leaves near them that alleviate stings. This sort of thinking held up in English rural areas until Wallace reported that things were actually a bit different in the tropics. There, durian fruits fall from the trees, and crush the skull of anyone taking a nap underneath. God doesn't provide a remedy for that. Perhaps God's goodness didn't extend to the tropics.'

He is referring to the explorer Alfred Russel Wallace, who corresponded with Darwin, supported and later opposed him, and developed similar theories of evolution at more or less the same time.

'Albert Schweitzer tried to run a tropical hospital along Christian principles. But if you don't kill mosquitoes, don't combat bacteria and don't chase away snakes, your chances of survival are slim. You first have to do battle with God's creatures before you can start to praise His principles.'

Were you an angry unbeliever?

'In the beginning I was angry because it was so clear that my parents' lives were based on a lie.'

They really believed in God; they weren't being hypocritical?

'No, they really believed.'

And did you try to convince them that they were wrong?

'Briefly. Atheism was too offensive for them to take seriously.'

I suddenly realise why chaos becomes more enjoyable as soon as I am travelling. There is much less of it. Or rather, there is much less chaos in me, and more chaos outside. And that external chaos is, to deliberately misparaphrase Darwin, delectable chaos. Interior chaos is not always delectable.

We drive silently past Redmond's old school.

He does not explain why we are not stopping. I do not remind him that the school is on our list. His list, actually. In everyday life I abhor lists.

'We'll stop there tomorrow,' he volunteers after a while. 'Did you see the hedge? That dates from my day.'

Did you have a hand in planting it?

'Yes.'

He reflects for a moment, and pouts demonstratively. 'More than just a hand, in fact. I laboured hard on it.

Military training formed part of the school curriculum, again inspired by the notion that we were preparing for a role in the Empire, and possibly a career in the army. During one of our drills I was put in charge of a platoon that I was supposed to lead into battle. Off we went, in uniform – I still remember how uncomfortable it was, how painfully it chafed – with real rifles, loaded with blanks. I couldn't follow the map; map reading was not my forte even then, and so I couldn't find the battle. I thought, let's just not show up then, and grant the opposition their victory. I led my platoon to a pub near Silbury Hill – that was always easy enough to find. We put our packs down outside along with the fifteen or twenty Lee-Enfield rifles, which we stacked neatly together. We ate chips and had a pint or two. Just then the major, a professional soldier who was responsible for the exercise, came in. He was incensed and yelled, "What the hell do you think you're doing?" When he had calmed down enough to speak normally, it turned out that he was chiefly angry that we had left our rifles outside. What if someone had pinched them? No one had, but the episode marked the end of my command.

He had a point, actually. Even without bullets the rifles could do some damage. A resourceful boy had once fired a sharpened pencil with one, killing a calf. His parents had to compensate the farmer, which the boy thought was unfair. Who could have thought that a mere pencil could be a lethal weapon?

I was genuinely interested in the army and might have considered a military career, but I obviously wasn't cut out for it. By way of alternative I was made to plant the hedge. And it's still there, I'm proud to say.'

Between Marlborough and Calne lies Silbury Hill, a prehistoric man-made mound 130-feet high, the tallest of its kind in Europe, and Avebury, whose stone circles are thought to pre-date Stonehenge by some five centuries. The pub where Redmond rested his troops has gone, though he can point out exactly where it stood.

Redmond prefers Avebury to Stonehenge, because it has more stones. Besides the circle, it boasts an ancient avenue arranged in pairs of male and female stones. It has been less sanitised for tourists, allowing the imagination a freer rein. He likes to think that Romans sold antique souvenirs here in their day. It is easy to picture orgies, fertility rites and rituals involving the sun, but perhaps those ancient inhabitants just used the spot for picnics, music and sport. Maybe it was the setting for the Isle of Wight Festival of its day. Or perhaps someone just had the crazy idea of standing as many stones on end as possible.

'The site remains a mystery. We don't know why the mound was built, only that it was clearly hugely important to its builders.'

The Red Lion, the pub in which he was hoping to spend the night, even serves Belgian beer these days, but has stopped providing accommodation. Perhaps not permanently, but at least for tonight. It doesn't matter. Redmond has already got another hotel in mind, in Calne itself, at a spot where his family used to dine once a term.

Avebury was the traditional destination for a family outing. Redmond's father objected to Darwin on many counts, but he was well-disposed to prehistory. The heathens that roamed England back in those days had not, after all, had the opportunity to learn about or reject Jesus. They had no alternative to paganism. His father was interested in archaeology, and had a theory about long heads and round heads.

'He'd read a lot on this subject and he was convinced there were two types of people: the original population and a hardy strain of migrants that had invaded Europe. Naturally, his theory was that the inhabitants of Calne were descendants of the primitive original inhabitants, the ones who worshipped the stones, and that that was why his church was almost deserted. I can't remember any more whether they had round heads or long heads. I think they had long heads. According to my father, they only lived in the vicinity of megaliths. I believe the thinking was that the round heads were better suited to wearing helmets, which gave them a military advantage.'

His father entertained a half-jokey, half-genuine fear of Avebury.

'Vicars didn't last long here. Two or three years at most. Because of its ghosts. Clergymen went mad in Avebury.'

At the church I read aloud from a gravestone, 'Loved by all who knew him.'

Redmond retorts promptly and sceptically, 'And absolutely detested by everyone else. Dear old Avebury. I came here often. It was a short cycle ride, both from school and Calne. Between its stones there was always a moment when I felt overwhelmed: a wow moment. Later it was more, wow man, far out.'

That echo of a hippy past resonates more strongly at the next location he wants to show me: West Kennet Long Barrow, for which the hiking boots have been brought along. One small problem arises, though. Although this prehistoric site is only a stone's throw from Avebury, we get lost en route. We zigzag back and forth down country lanes. At each crossing he asks me which turning I would take. We usually favour different directions. After a good half-hour we have bridged the stone's throw. The hiking boots prove unnecessary: the path to the site has long been levelled and cleared of mud.

'I knew it,' growls Redmond disappointedly. 'We're lucky they haven't set up souvenir stalls.'

The path bears testimony to past visitors. We pass faded scraps of cloth and coins that have been hammered into tree trunks. Like Avebury, West Kennet Long Barrow is something of a mystery, but is thought to be a prehistoric burial site, possibly containing the graves of generations of a prominent family. According to local legend, the barrow is visited at the solstice by a spirit robed in white.

As a student, Redmond came here with a few hippy friends.

Somebody had come up with the idea of sacrificing a chicken. 'The idea being that we would leave the chicken for the spirits. Whatever spirits those were. But then again we weren't spaced out enough – or sufficiently well off – to stick to our plan, so we just took the slaughtered chicken home and ate it.'

He feels a sense of kinship with prehistoric man, seeing his life as a writer as a mockery of the kind of existence those distant ancestors had.

'That's why I write at night. I'd often wondered why everything became much more interesting at night. Then I developed a theory. It comes down to the fact that, as a man, you really shouldn't be spending your days behind a desk – and you certainly shouldn't be in the women's cave. You should be outdoors, driving mammoths over a cliff. Male writers are often troubled by a subliminal awareness that they should be hunting, and overcome their shame in many different ways. Proust wrote at night and in bed. Dostoevsky gambled away all his money before he turned to writing. Tolstoy worked at a desk during the day, but compensated by dressing as a peasant; he looked as though he would be off at any minute to labour in the fields. He forced himself to work for twelve hours at a stretch, longer than the average peasant. Nabokov could only write standing up. Or – another interesting fact – he would sit in his car writing on index cards held against his steering wheel as if he was on the point of departure. The man who wrote The Leopard, Lampedusa, wrote at a local café. He was a prince, who went to the café for amusement, not for his work. So if he wrote there, it didn't count as work. Balzac wrote at night, in a dressing gown, a sort of monk's habit; he actually thought of himself as a monk. Men need an excuse to be able to write. I need the night. In that respect women are privileged. They can sit down at their writing desks in the middle of performing household chores without any sense of conflict.'

We walk back to the car. No more excursions can be devised. We must really start inching our way into Calne.

Feeling a bit queasy, perhaps?

'Oh, the whole time. But actually it's not as bad as I'd feared.'

How long ago is it since you were here last?

'An eternity. I never wanted to come back because I thought it would destroy my ability to write. Memories are so valuable. The new things that you see threaten the images that are stored in your head.'

We enter the little town through a poor neighbourhood.

'Round heads, I think, though that man's pulling a long face.'

He steers the Clio into the car park of the hotel he has chosen: Lansdowne Strand. His main memory is of the hotel bar, which features impressive wainscoting and displays of china.

The hotel turns out to have been taken over by the Best Western chain. But it has not yet succumbed to all mediocre norms. The car park is partially hemmed in by sheds. There is no lift. It is too homely. Too illogical. The smell of cleaning fluids is too overpowering. The first thing I do is imprison myself in my room. I have activated a locking mechanism that I cannot undo. The key only works from the outside. There isn't even a keyhole on the inside. The room telephone does not work. I resort to ringing reception with my mobile. 'Please hold the line ...' For about four minutes I listen to one of the *Four Seasons*. I try again.

To his credit, the receptionist does run swiftly upstairs.

'It's incredible how often this happens,' he says in a somewhat reproachful tone, because he has other things to do. 'When you pull the key out of the lock you need to check what position it's in. If you get it wrong, you lock yourself in.'

So why doesn't he or his manager change the system?

'That's a good question, to which I don't have a good answer. But if you get stuck again, just use the house telephone. That's what it's there for. And it's free.'

It doesn't work.

'Are you sure? I'll look into it immediately.'

Redmond has not had any such problems. After failing to find me in the lobby, he quickly relocated to the bar and is happily scrutinising the hotel and bar customers, counting heads and dividing them into long and round specimens. 'Christ, that one's round all right.' He enjoys the rough banter of the bar clientele and the fleeting contacts between them and their wives, who come every now and then to check that their better half is still upright. Opposite the hotel is a brand new, impressive-looking library.

'Well, well, well. Things are looking up. Books!'

The library has taken the place of what, in Redmond's youth, was Calne's leading business: Harris Pork and Bacon, the main local employer and centre of the town's economy. The factory shut down operations in 1983.

'My mother called Calne a "pig town".' He puts on a high, querulous voice, '"I could have been an actress, but now I'm doomed to live in a pig town." The factory produced pork pies and sausages. Pigs brought a degree of prosperity to a place that was predominantly poor.'

Did your mother have the talent to be an actress?

'It's impossible to say. She was firmly convinced that she could have enjoyed a brilliant career. That conviction was never tested or disproved by failure, though; she never made the attempt. She was crazy about drama; it filled her with energy and enthusiasm. Her greatest professional moment was a role in the chorus at the world premiere of *Murder in the Cathedral*. T.S. Eliot signed her copy of the script, to which she herself had added stage directions. But her career was over by the time she married. She had seen my father in Guildford Cathedral in his RAF uniform.' Again he imitates a high, complaining voice, '"Girls just are defenceless against a man in uniform. My heart went a-boom, a-boom. And I've rued it ever since."

A nice thing for a child to hear, eh? But of course I can't blame her for being stage-struck. She compensated for the loss of an acting career in her own way. She managed to get the butcher, the baker, the bricklayer, the stonemasons and the postmistress to take part in mystery plays. I remember her prodding a poor sick farmer onto the stage. She did manage to put on some kind of performance every year and that enabled her to cling on to her past in a small way. One of her plays was staged at St Paul's Cathedral and was very well reviewed. With the exception of the electric lighting, everything was just as in the Middle Ages. People spoke in a local dialect that was very hard to understand. Many of the players had never been to London before. She had a room full of costumes and props. I still have a cloth fish that was used for the miracle of the loaves and fishes.'

Was she religious?

'Yes, in the unquestioning way of a typical convert. After her death I read some of her diary entries. She hoped to be reunited with her mother in heaven. She expected all the dogs that she had had in her lifetime to greet her at the pearly gates. She had written down all their names. It wasn't the kind of faith you could reason against; it was purely emotional. I don't think she entertained the slightest doubt.'

He sips his bitter and tears his eyes away from the round and long heads, who are following a televised football match.

'She beat me quite often. Sometimes she beat me so hard that I fainted. Once, when I came round, I dragged myself to my father's study. It was cold, so I went and sat by the gas fire, next to the old spaniel that would nip me when I didn't watch out. I got too close and my jumper caught fire. At that moment my father turned round and called, "Kate! Kate!", but didn't move a muscle. My mother came running up and smothered the flames with cushions. She kissed me and cuddled me, pressing me to her bosom and calling me her "little darling". Less than half an hour after she'd beaten me. I thought, never trust emotions like that.'

Did she remember how she had treated you?

'Oh yes, of course. She would get angry, hysterical even, and then beat me. Then almost immediately afterwards she would be as nice as pie. It was a lightning transformation. She was also a great dissembler. You could identify visitors to our house from some way off. When the doorbell went she would say, "That awful little man's back," then open the door and welcome the awful little man attentively. "How good to see you, Mr Atkins. Do come in. We were just talking about you." The man in question would be in a terrible mess, his wife would have run off, taking the children, his life would be in tatters. That's the thing about a vicarage; the door is always open, but our visitors couldn't count on sympathy, and certainly not on friendship. Hypocrisy, on the other hand, was never in short supply.

When I lived in Oxford many years later and looked Belinda

up, she said, "How good to see you." I thought, give her five minutes and she'll soon change her tune. Just as my mother always said one thing in the presence of outsiders and quite another when she was with us. So I only spent five minutes with Belinda, and then fled on my motorbike. That's probably why she thought I was special. Arrggghh.'

Did Belinda manage to cure you of that suspicion?

'Eventually. To a degree. A few days ago I visited her in hospital. She was exhausted and said, "You're behaving as you used to do forty years ago."'

You escape before things get painful?

'Something like that. I have learned never to show my true feelings. I expect to be lied to. It's difficult to be cured of hypocrisy.'

Did your father beat you too?

'Never. But he also never hugged me or kissed me. It was just out of the question.'

Dusk is falling. Calne, a little town of around 15,000 souls, looks innocent enough. The library disturbs Redmond's memories. Not only has the pork factory gone, so has the smell of meat. But you can't overlook the church. In fact, you can see two churches.

Calne has had its share of illustrious residents. Joseph Priestley settled here in 1773 to pursue his scientific investigations after having made the discovery that plants produce oxygen. By placing a mouse under a jar by itself, then putting another mouse under a jar together with a plant, he was able to prove that the latter lived longer. Shortly afterwards, in 1779, another resident of Calne, the Dutchman Jan Ingenhousz, made the further discovery that sunlight was necessary if the plant was to save the mouse from suffocation.

Redmond was aware of Priestley's experiments, but is surprised by the plaque in Church Street commemorating Ingenhousz's discovery. He does, however, know of another historic connection in the same street, with Samuel Taylor Coleridge. 'Coleridge lived here for a year or two. He wrote his *Biographia Literaria* in Calne. At the time he was on the run from his creditors, and no one was prepared to pursue him this far. William Cobbett, who travelled through Calne in the early nineteenth century, claimed that it was the dirtiest town he'd ever set foot in.' Cobbett edited a weekly newspaper called *The Register*, aimed at the labouring man. He travelled extensively in rural England and published an account of his travels, the famous *Rural Rides*. Later he became a Radical member of Parliament.

Would you like such a plaque?

'Fervently. I don't care where, and care even less what's on it. I'd be happy with one in the vicarage lavatory.'

"He loved bitter?"

'That would be perfect.'

The houses and streets have a pastel hue, though that may be the effect of the dusk. Mellow bricks, Bath Stone, cobblestones.

Is Calne old?

'There was a settlement here in the tenth century. The church held a synod here to pronounce on the celibacy of the clergy. During the debate the floor collapsed. Archbishop Dunstan, who was standing above a beam, survived, but the opponents of celibacy were killed or injured by falling timber. That was seen as a sign that he had God on his side.'

Redmond is distracted by a passer-by.

'Now he definitely had a long head.'

We walk past the first church, the Free Church.

'They were stricter than us. There weren't any Roman Catholics in Calne.'

The Anglican Church is locked.

'In my day the gate was always open.'

Each house sets off a memory.

'Here was where I had my first smoochy dance as a teenager – and here they used to grind wheat. It smelt heavenly. Each shop, each house had its own smell. Do you see the supermarket down there? It used to be a cinema, and the owner would complain about the church bells disturbing his screenings. My father said, "If you can prove that the cinema was there before the church, I will have the bells silenced." He could surprise me occasionally. It used to flood here every now and then. My father kept ducks; he would let them come down to the stream. It delighted him that other people would feed his birds. It didn't cost him a penny! In the evening we had to go and round up the ducks. And this is the Doctor's Pond, where Joseph Priestley discovered oxygen.'

The church and the vicarage are about a hundred yards apart. The vicarage is huge, more like a small, walled castle.

'The wall is falling into disrepair now. We lived in isolation from the rest of the world. From our garden I would walk in my Wellington boots to the river. I would turn over stones looking for miller's thumbs – have you ever heard of them?' It turns out that they are fish, also known as bullheads. 'They're small, with a broad flat head, and as fast as lightning. You see one and then woof, off it's gone; you can never catch them. At the time I assumed that the name referred to the mill.'

Given Redmond's strong reluctance to visit the place, I had pictured hellish surroundings, but this seems a beautiful spot in which to grow up.

'Well it was. But ...'

He interrupts himself in mid mental leap.

'A kingfisher! Did you see it?'

Missed it.

Did your father ever have any reservations about the privileged life he led?

'No, he thought that he was entitled to it all. The man of God was a cut above the rest. He was a local dignitary; lived a bit like a squire. The BBC rang him up to ask how Calne should be pronounced – the vicar was seen as an authority on such matters. On the other hand, he didn't own his own home and couldn't afford to heat it.'

Midges swarm above his head; possibly above my head, too. I point this out to him.

He is untroubled.

'Midges need warmth and altitude to mate. They're only thinking about sex, so we needn't worry about getting bitten.'

He points to a gateway at the rear. 'I used to lie on the wide flat top of the wall there and read. It seemed so secret and special. My mother would call me. "Reddy." I loathed that. Or "Redsi", which I preferred. There were hens wandering about all over the place. We had wonderful bird books at home. My father also had a library of philosophical and theological works, and he read a great deal about what used to be called Abyssinia – he wrote a monograph on the Coptic Church. The windows have been replaced: they have metal frames now. They used to be wood.'

Shall we see if they'll let us in?

'They'll want to show us the house.'

That's good, isn't it?

'It might make it even more difficult for me to recreate how it was. They've done it up.'

Shall I ring the doorbell?

'Better not. It's quite late already. They'll be having dinner. You know we lived here for twenty years. We had an enormous lawn, with tall trees dotted about. Taller than these. The fact that I wasn't here that often made it even more special. My father was transferred here when I was about four, so this was the place where I grew up. When Belinda came to visit much later, we had to dress for dinner. Put on a tie. The silver was laid out. Belinda found it daunting.'

He looks from the vicarage wall to the town centre and back with a somewhat confounded air.

'I must admit ... it no longer looks Dickensian. The poorest of the poor have vanished. Relations are less feudal.

My best friend was Timmy Atwell, the milkman's son. He often had to help his father, for instance by washing bottles. We both loved Dinky toys. He had a tanker lorry and lots of milk floats, and I had tanks. My parents had decided to send me to a prep school in Dorset. I said, "Timmy, you must come with me." When my parents heard that, an embarrassed silence ensued, because this was of course out of the question. The son of a milkman could never afford to go to a school like that. Though they did help to get him in some alternative school.

Timmy, I and some others formed a kind of gang. One day we decided that a red-haired girl called Linda, the daughter of the local constable, needed to be taught a lesson. All six of us marched up to her, with me at the head, firmly convinced we would beat her up, but she folded her arms on her chest and taunted us, "Try it if you dare." I turned round to see that all my followers had fled. I had to run after them. Since then I have never even entertained the idea of opposing a woman.'

The days of the gang were numbered.

'When I was about twelve, I was forbidden to play any longer with the local boys. I was to consort with boys of my class.'

On the way back to the hotel Redmond suddenly realises that he forgot to tell me about the most important episode at the vicarage.

'I must have been about four and a half. I was playing on the lawn next to the sundial when suddenly a bird's egg fell to the ground in front of me. It was a mistle thrush's egg – or rather half an eggshell. I thought that God had given me a present. Or that the present came from the bird. I was ecstatic. For the first time in my life I fully comprehended how wonderful birds were. I began to collect eggs. And I was placed in charge of the egg collection at my primary school. Every now and again I would purloin an egg from that collection and replace it with an egg of which I possessed two specimens. Then I would stick the label of the rare egg on a pigeon's egg. I wonder if they ever relabelled them ...'

Chapter 3

UNWILLINGLY TO SCHOOL

A pattern begins to emerge. As I wrestle with a kipper, Redmond urgently enquires, 'How's our list getting on?'

I dig it out. As a fully neutral observer I must conclude that it has not been a success. Of all the objectives that we noted down, only Calne has been achieved.

'So what didn't we cross off?'

Petrol, stamps, the roll of film, Marlborough College.

'We need to make a new list. We'll visit the school today.'

I guess we still need petrol.

'And we have to forward that letter pretty urgently.'

A small cloud of stress envelops us.

'What's the state of play regarding your room telephone?'

Still not fixed.

'It's all part of the package. Locking up guests. Seeing if they're resourceful enough to escape. There was a jacuzzi in my room. I wanted to try it out, but when I got in, I didn't know how to work it. So I just took an ordinary bath.'

Pelican House, Redmond's home

Though it does not lie on our route, we will have to return to Pelican House later today. Redmond has agreed to meet a journalist from *The New Yorker*, who is to interview him about his friend Ian McEwan.

But first he takes me to a place that isn't on our new list. We make our way to a little church, a mile or so from Calne, one of the three churches at which his father had to hold Sunday services. Redmond overtakes a couple of horsewomen on a bumpy lane with practised ease. 'I'm a real country boy.' He enters the church with a hesitant air.

'It still looks exactly the same. It even smells exactly the same.'

A board gives the numbers of the hymns to be sung at the next service.

'We sometimes had to go with him on Sundays, and sit through the same sermon again. And when I saw all the hymns on the board I would think, this is going to take a while. Yet another hour for me to let my thoughts run wild.'

His father, he says, was not what you would call a gifted preacher.

'He used the model sermons distributed by the diocese. He would start to hold forth about the Holy Ghost, but tended to get distracted, especially if he was doing it for the third time that day. He would say that he was going to discuss four points, and would start off spiritedly, but his thoughts would gradually begin to wander to the lawnmower, which was in urgent need of repair. Then he would forget what the third or fourth point was and have to play for time by getting out his handkerchief and blowing his nose. That didn't help him to remember the fourth point, but by then the faithful had also been distracted or had dozed off, or had even forgotten that there was supposed to be a fourth point.'

Was he funny, did he have a sense of humour?

'No.'

We drive down a lane. He gestures sketchily at the rolling fields to the left. Somewhere near there, the Cavaliers and Roundheads fought during the Civil War.

'I used to take girls up that hill. It never worked. I always picked the wrong ones. Girls who knew who my father was and were sure he wouldn't approve of me getting anywhere near their underwear.'

In the years before those doomed attempts to get off with girls, he used to take Hubert, the family dog, up here. Hubert was old and fat; he was always keen to go on a walk, but after a few steps he got tired and wanted to be carried. Hubert was uncompromising: if nobody was prepared to carry him, he would ostentatiously lie down and refuse to budge. A typical family excursion would see O'Hanlon senior holding forth on such topics as archaeology, plants and animals and the Civil War, while Redmond vainly tried to urge the unresponsive Hubert onwards.

Redmond suddenly realises that he will have to talk about Ian McEwan later in the day and starts to dredge up memories. 'One day, Ian and I walked here from Marlborough. He then called a taxi to take us back, a distance of some thirty miles or so. The cab driver had never had such a lucrative fare. On our walks he always outpaces me, while I struggle to keep up. I feel as if I'm running, whereas from his point of view we're dawdling. Ian is very competitive: he's in superb shape.'

En route Redmond has seen something that intrigues him: the Atwell-Wilson Motor Museum. He conjectures that it has been set up by his boyhood friend Timmy, reasoning that his love of Dinky toys must have evolved into a love of old-timers. We turn back. Redmond parks in front of the museum, a grey barrack in a back garden.

'It's shut – and a good thing too,' says Redmond. 'We don't have time for this anyway.'

'Hello!'

A white-haired old lady peers round the doorpost of her house. She sports a green eyeshade of the kind worn by newspaper editors in old films and is plucking at a pair of rubber gloves. They resist her attempts to remove them, so she keeps them on. When she catches sight of Redmond, her agitation visibly diminishes. This is a side of him that I had not suspected: he reassures people, despite his wild side whiskers and sweeping, clumsy gestures. She introduces herself as Hasell.

'Good morning. The museum only opens at eleven, I'm afraid. Richard, my husband, has had a fall and I am giving him a massage.'

The eyeshade and the rubber gloves lend the massage a certain *je ne sais quoi*.

Redmond asks if the museum is owned by Timmy Atwell.

'No. Tim is Richard's nephew. My sister married Tim's father. So although I'm a Wilson, there are Atwells on both sides of the family.'

If we do not nip this in the bud, we will be treated to an account of the entire family tree.

Redmond is unconcerned. 'Mary Jane,' he suggests. He says the name affectionately.

'Do you know Mary Jane? She's my niece, not my sister.'

'We used to dance at her farm some three hundred years ago. Please give her my best wishes.'

'And who are you?'

'My father was the vicar here for twenty-eight years. O'Hanlon. I'm Redmond.'

'You're Reverend O'Hanlon?'

'No.' Redmond turns the volume up, 'I'm his son. Redmond. I used to play with Tim. Timmy and Reddy, inseparable companions. We had a wonderful collection of Dinky toys and I thought that he must have gone on to collect full-size cars.'

'No, Richard and I built up the museum together.'

What happened to Tim?

'He lives in Bognor Regis now. He's an accountant.'

'Didn't he go to New York for a while?'

'You're mixing him up with James, Richard's brother. James is the Dean of Winchester Cathedral. He was in the United States, at Harvard and various other places. What do you do?'

'I got into the habit of travelling to jungles and of trying to die there. Well, I always stopped just short of dying, because I wanted to come back to write about it. That's been my life.'

Hasell pushes back her eyeshade so that she can scratch her scalp.

'Shall I let you into the museum anyway? Even if it isn't anywhere near opening time?'

'Don't bother,' Redmond says, 'another time would be better, we're sort of in a hurry.'

'And I'd better get back to Richard. He'll be getting cramp by now.'

Redmond walks happily back to the car. He doesn't know what pleases him most. Hasell's eyeshade (an editor's hat, as he puts it) or the memory of Mary Jane.

She'll talk about you for days, I say.

'I hope so.' He imitates Hasell's voice quite convincingly, '"Are you Reverend ...?" No, I'm Redmond. I think she's still confusing me with my father.'

He starts the car.

'Mary Jane was a farmer's daughter. I would sometimes go to her farm, just as I would go to other farms. She was tall, very dark and hairy.'

And you were in love with the farmer's daughter?

'Not exactly. But her tallness, darkness and hairiness cast a certain spell ...

As a boy, my friend James, who was a farmer's son and is now apparently a big shot at Winchester Cathedral, was incredibly dim. It was in the vicarage, with James, that I first appreciated the power of storytelling. I made up a story about a terrifying spectre that was sometimes seen in the vicarage cellar. And if the ghostly gong sounded, you knew it was about to appear. I locked James in the cellar and then banged the gong which was used to announce mealtimes. After waiting for a while, I unlocked the cellar door. James emerged, as white as a sheet. He'd fallen for it hook, line and sinker. The power of literature at work! Not long afterwards he decided that he did not want to take over his parents' farm. Instead he wanted to become a priest. To think that it was I who introduced him to the spirit world! I still feel guilty about it.'

We drive past a caravan which is being drawn by a horse. Redmond tries to make out whether it contains gypsies or hippies. Both categories of traveller make caravans intriguing to him.

I think I spot an unusual bird sitting on top of the vehicle.

'That's a crow.'

A common crow?

'Yes, but in territory like this crows display a considerable sense of humour. If there is a buzzard nearby, they imitate the buzzard. If they see a red kite, they mimic that. So it's a crow that isn't itself.'

His thoughts return to James, the dim Dean of Winchester. 'My father had persuaded another farmer's boy to take the cloth. But in his case I could understand it. He'd had enough of getting up at the crack of dawn on winter mornings to milk the cows. He was better off becoming a priest. It's a much easier life.'

Still thinking of farmers, he tells me about a local pond that was used as a cache for smuggled brandy. 'One day the customs officer was coming past and saw some men gazing intently at the pond. "What are you doing?" he asked. "We're looking at the reflection of the moon," they replied. "So that's what farmers get up to in their spare time, eh?" the official allegedly retorted, amused by such rural simplicity.'

A white horse has been cut out of the turf on a hill near the road.

'Ian and I came past here on our walking trip. We had smoked some dope and the monument seemed to keep changing position. Dope apparently galvanises it. It has the opposite effect on me: it makes all my energy drain out of my heels.'

Troubled memories are gradually starting to well up about his old school, Marlborough College, which tops our list for today.

'I had a knee operation and was out of action for quite a long time. The injury happened during a rugby match. I was a right-prop, being sturdy. The housemaster had played for England and sport was the only thing he cared about. I made the mistake of pushing him in the scrum; he pushed back, probably in a reflex reaction, and broke my knee.'

Was he at all ashamed?

'Not really. I think he felt bad about it briefly, because he was nice to me for a time. He visited me in hospital, and later took me to that pub at Silbury Hill. He would also buy me a meal there after he'd beaten me. In a way that made it worse.'

How often were you beaten?

'Quite often at prep school. Only about three times at Marl-borough. One of my crimes was smoking or drinking during prep, for which I got six strokes of the cane. It was always six strokes of the cane. You knew that you were going to get beaten:

Redmond O'Hanlon (back row, third from left) and his hockey teammates at Marlborough College

the anticipation was probably worse than the pain. He would come to get you around midnight. You were sore for a couple of days afterwards.

Rugby is terrible: a brutal game that provides a grounding in man-to-man combat – it's a form of military training, really. We had organised sports every afternoon, of course, to keep impure thoughts at bay. To keep boys from onanism. That's what masturbation used to be called. The official line was that it weakened you and eventually made you go blind.'

The broken knee had its good side. His biology teacher, Jack Halliday, gave him private lessons during the holiday. 'I would go to Marlborough on my motorbike. I think my parents paid him, though it can't have been much. I had him all to myself, which was as it always should have been. No other nasty boys. I think he was about sixty; he died not long afterwards.

Biology was by far my favourite subject; unfortunately I was useless at chemistry and maths, though. In the hope of scraping through algebra I devised a technique that involved writing notes on my sleeves and making an impression of them on paper at the beginning of an exam. Unfortunately the impression proved too faint to be legible. I wasn't even any good at cheating. During the chemistry exam I would see others writing away effortlessly while I sweated, unable to distinguish one formula from another. I could hear sparrows cheeping scornfully outside, as if to say "What an idiot". That was the final straw, as far as I was concerned; even the sparrows were laughing at me. I switched to English with only a term to go, since that was a subject that anybody could do. I got the best marks for biology that Jack had ever given: an A1, as it was then called. When I switched subjects he was extremely disappointed, saying, "That's a great loss to science." I explained to him that I didn't have any alternative, that I just couldn't do maths. "Nor can I," he said. In his day you didn't have to. The course that he taught at Marlborough was still the one devised in the nineteenth century by T.H. Huxley, the man they called Darwin's bulldog. It was a beautiful course, in which everything had meaning: insects, reptiles, amphibians, birds, mammals.'

So you were taught about evolution?

'Certainly. The English teacher had painted murals in the lab about the evolution of life on earth. Jack Halliday went to chapel, perhaps he even believed in God, but he always held his prayer book upside down. He was a real hero to me. The fact that he was so fat lent him extra authority in my eyes. Though he had to join in the hymn singing in chapel – otherwise he would have lost his job.'

Did he ever talk about God?

'Oh, good heavens no. It was a school founded on religious principles; teachers couldn't express doubts, assuming they had them. But his teaching said enough. Never accept anything as fact just because it comes from the voice of authority: that was the point he would always stress. Never take anything on trust, not even from the most eminent scientists. He would add, "And the same thing goes for anything I say". If you can't back a theory with experiments, it is probably flawed. That's what we were taught in biology. Whereas the headmaster would tell us to respect our elders and never to question the authority of the Church. My father did the same. What a ridiculous commandment: honour thy father and mother. If everyone took that to heart, science would never progress. Wouldn't that be appalling? So sod the idea of putting progenitors on a pedestal.

Biology overturned all these precepts, which is another reason why I found it so exciting.'

But the course of your life was determined in your final term?

'In the sense that I opted to study English, so that I could write about biology. In a way that was the perfect combination. Whatever happens later in life, we always return to the things that appealed to us in our youth. Francis Galton said that, and it certainly applies to me.'

Galton, a cousin of Darwin's, is one of Redmond's heroes.

'He takes at least half the credit for resolving the issue of religion for me. Galton wondered what the difference was between Christianity, with its churches and crucifixes, and idol worship, with its fetishes and spirit houses. He carried out an experiment to see if he could conjure up religious feelings by worshipping the most unlikely idol he could think of, eventually opting for the figure of Mr Punch. He cut out a picture of Punch, framed it and put it on his desk. Over a period of six weeks he knelt before the idol and prayed to it ten times a day. He concluded that he was wasting his time and that it was having no effect at all. But then he went to his club, and after lunch to the club library, where his eye fell on a copy of *Punch*, featuring the image of Mr Punch on its cover. He started to sweat; he suddenly felt faint and unwell, and had to leave. In that same instant he realised that the conditioning had worked. He immediately cancelled his subscription to the journal.'

After Redmond's guffaw has died away, he proceeds to extol Galton's many achievements. He anticipated and later inspired Freud, with his painstaking exploration of the human subconscious. 'He was a polymath; his only failing was that he sometimes abandoned his topics of research too quickly. Then he would turn to another field, like statistics. He invented a device called the clicker, a pocket recording device with which he tried to make a "beauty map" of Great Britain, rating women as beautiful, middling or ugly. He concluded that the women of London were ten per cent prettier than those of Edinburgh. That finding didn't lead to a scientific breakthrough, but he did discover the existence of anticyclones and he pioneered the use of fingerprinting in criminal investigations.

He was also enthusiastic about the work being done by his cousin, Charles Darwin, and hoped to help him with his investigation into inheritance mechanisms. He, like Darwin, believed that your characteristics, even your dirty thoughts, were transmitted to the next generation through particles called gemmules, that were shed by your organs and carried by the blood to the reproductive cells. Galton transfused blood between black and white rabbits, expecting them to produce grey offspring. Instead they fell ill, then went on producing black and white offspring. Darwin wasn't too thrilled.'

As we drive through the gates of Marlborough College, its grandeur unfolds, revealing a semicircular, neoclassical building with stone columns: the Memorial Hall, where the pupils assemble on special occasions. Redmond once played Hamlet on its stage. 'The fastest Hamlet in history. I loved the sword fighting.'

Did you shine in your role?

'Not really. I was supposed to be the star of the show, but I was overshadowed by a freckled boy who played Ophelia. Ordinarily you wouldn't look twice at him, but once he'd got his costume on he was transformed; you didn't notice his freckles anymore. God, the bastard was talented! People couldn't take their eyes off him; the leading man might as well have been part of the scenery.'

Though that is an achievement of sorts, being the fastest.

'I dare say.'

No silences, no pauses?

'None. Why should you drag something out if you can say it quickly?'

His eye falls on the building that was his sanctuary in former days.

'Gosh. They've painted the laboratories. They used to be green; now they're white.'

He parks the car on a quadrangle at the rear of the school and shows me the athletics track. 'I used to loathe athletics.'

Were there any sports that you did like?

'Not really. Certainly not rugby. Hockey wasn't too bad. I was quite fast in those days. There was target practice too, of course. The rifles used to be kept in the building on the other side of the car park.'

That turns out still to be the case.

'There are rucksacks outside.'

But no rifles.

Nowadays, a keen female officer is in charge of the school's military activities.

'There is a new rifle range,' she says, as if this is what we want to know. 'It's twenty-five yards long.' Redmond blames his deafness on the target practice sessions at school. 'We had no hearing protection whatever, and I spent a lot of time at the rifle range. Everyone did. It was an indoor range, so the din was incredible.' These days pupils are equipped with ear muffs and the range is much longer.

Redmond tells the story about his friend who killed a calf with a pencil. The pencil is mightier than the sword.

'Oh,' the officer says. 'I know that story. So it's true?'

I begin to tell about the time that Redmond missed the battle. He takes over the narrative with gusto.

'I haven't heard that one before,' she says.

'Mmm,' mumbles Redmond, perhaps somewhat crest-fallen that his adventures have not entered school mythology. Unlike the pencil and calf.

We walk on. The school buildings encircle an artificial mound that may be as ancient as Silbury Hill, that is to say older than Stonehenge. We arrive at the main quad, near the dining hall, where the pupils, boys and girls, but mainly boys, are playing with a dog. Many of them are texting or making telephone calls during their break.

'That dog makes it more humane.'

I already find the school quite humane, light years away from the terrible regime described by Redmond.

'They all look healthy and wealthy.'

In his fourth year at Marlborough Redmond breached the

rules by riding a motorcycle on the school campus and was expelled.

'It happened a week or so before the end of term. I got my Royal Enfield Crusader 250cc, tuned it to make the maximum racket, drove through the school gates and then in circles round this quad. At places like this people don't panic, but the chaplain did run upstairs to ring the porter, who trudged off and started to close the gate. I shot through just in the nick of time.

The headmaster told me I was a roué, a degenerate, and that I would certainly be dead before I was thirty.'

How old were you then?

'Too young, actually. I was a year younger than my class-mates. That sounds good, but it put me at a disadvantage. I was the weakest: everyone was older and tougher than me. I must have been seventeen or just short of it. In those days you could get a motorcycle licence when you turned sixteen.

They couldn't chuck me out on the spot, because it would have meant losing their Hamlet. I was given permission to stay until the last performance. Then I had to go. My mother came to watch the play. I don't think my father ever showed up.'

He is somewhat taken aback by the relaxed air that the school projects. The boys are wearing blazers and ties, or tracksuits. The older girls wear long black skirts, while the younger ones have knee-length kilts.

'It's the girls that make the difference. They're so sexy.'

Many of them have bare midriffs. Their plunging necklines must be breaking some rule or other. They wear make-up and piercings.

'And look at all those sporty types. They have the same swagger, exactly the same self-assured air as in my day. We wore ties too, though we also had starched collars and starched shirt cuffs. Our shirts were only washed once a week, but the starched extremities gave the illusion of cleanliness.'

He gives an impromptu commentary. I tape his voice, but feel the lack of a camera team.

'There used to be lime trees here. Here you could buy textbooks. We never wanted to sit in this little park ... It was so depressing. It's still depressing. Even the teachers look young, now. They're younger than I am.'

The pupils, by contrast, look strangely old, as if they have already assumed their adult forms.

'Yes, it's strange. They are being robbed of their youth. They are already bankers. They just don't know yet that the banks are collapsing. I see they now also have an official sports kit; we used to just wear a shirt and a pair of shorts. You still see the same kind of characters walking around. That curly-headed blond boy is clearly top in sports. I remember his type from all those years ago. The kind who were dominant, who walked with the confident tread of the victor. No sense of humour and not very bright.'

We enter a complex of buildings.

'This was the sixth-form library. It's just as it was, except for the computers. It's still a lovely place. I used to like to sit here.'

As we leave the library he quivers slightly with shock.

'Bloody hell. This is where we used to sit exams. And what do we see now? Flowers. Women's influence, I suppose. In my day no one would have dreamt of cheering things up with flowers. Everything is more civilised now that there are women around.'

He doesn't want to enter the dormitory, or rather, the place where the dormitory used to be. The queasiness is becoming too painful. 'And everything will be different, anyway; I don't want to disturb that memory.'

What did you do in the evenings?

'Nothing special. There was time for prep and then you went to bed. If I got the chance, I would sneak off to the lab.'

The corridor between the dormitory and the main library is hung with announcements about charities and fund-raising activities. There is also a poster for Les Misérables. 'Fenton is raking it in.' James Fenton, the poet with whom Redmond travelled to Borneo, contributed a few lines to the libretto of Les Misérables. It has made him a few millions.

If you scrape off the trauma, I say, the school doesn't seem too bad.

'Absolutely,' he grudgingly admits. 'Of course, we didn't have any flowers. I can't imagine what life would be like in a co-educational school. I would be constantly in love. The girls are all so attractive; they have that gloss that the children of wealthy people possess. The pupils exude prosperity. They look like film stars.'

We enter the main library.

Do you think they have your books here?

'I wouldn't think so. If you get chucked out, I assume your achievements are erased.'

The assistant librarian stops us. She looks strict, with shiny little glasses and her hair in a bun, and advances on us with the air of an angry cat, demanding to know whether we have permission to be on the premises. 'Or are you giving yourselves an unofficial tour?'

Unofficial is clearly a dirty word in her book.

But we keep her talking, to prevent Redmond from being thrown out all over again.

How many pupils are there now?

'Eight or nine hundred, I believe.'

'The same as in my day,' says Redmond.

'Nearly two years ago we got a new librarian, who has transformed the place. She'll be here in twenty minutes. Would you like to know how to make an appointment with her?'

We decline the offer.

'Did you at least report to the porter on arrival?'

Redmond explains that he's been on bad terms with the porter for almost half a century.

Are pupils still not allowed to ride motorcycles?

'No. They are not even allowed bicycles.'

'I noticed that,' says Redmond. 'The bike shed's disappeared.'

Why aren't they allowed bicycles?

'It is too distracting,' the woman says. 'The roads are too dangerous. Pupils are allowed out, but only during organised activities.'

Redmond says, somewhat plaintively, 'So many changes. Are pupils still beaten at least?'

The assistant librarian laughs reluctantly and humourlessly. 'Not officially, no.'

She doesn't seem to know what to think about our presence; she is tense and looks relieved when we make a move to leave. We are warned either to leave directly, or to ask the porter for permission to look round the school.

'God,' sighs Redmond, 'things were so different in my day. I'm shocked. No canings, no bicycles. But there are girls. Perhaps the two things are connected, and bicycles were banned when girls were admitted. Bikes make it easy to escape and do forbidden things.'

There seem to be enough hidden nooks around the school, and woods within walking distance.

'That's true, but you can make yourself scarce very quickly on a bicycle. The influence of women cannot be overestimated. You probably can't call the pupils by their surnames or their numbers anymore. Women don't hold with that kind of thing. Bullying probably takes different forms. Girls don't go in for as much physical violence, but they have other methods that are no less terrible. In my day the bullies tended to be the dimmer older boys lording it over the younger ones.'

And did no one protect the weak?

'No. I think the idea was: let them get on with it. It's good preparation for life – it'll get much worse in the army. They made the boys' lives hard in order to toughen them up. After prep school I only saw my parents for about fifteen weeks a year. This school is a mere twelve miles or so from my old home. I could easily have cycled there and back. But that was frowned on, so I never went home, except during the holidays.'

It sounds like torture.

'I think it was all part of the training. Subconsciously you feel abandoned by your parents – and because you don't see them so often, you can't develop much of a bond. They're probably relieved when you go off to school again. Since you're not at home much you have to create an alternative world. As a result, life in the army or the navy seems fine. People ask me if I was emotionally damaged. Of course I was damaged. Bloody hell. Belinda thought it strange that I was never able to cry. But it was just drummed into you: boys don't cry. Arrrgh! Nowadays, I practice. At night I howl. I think I'm starting to worry the neighbour's dog.'

We walk back to the car. He doesn't feel quite so desperately averse to the place now, he tells me in a sudden rush. His queasiness has largely gone. 'But if I come back, I will have to wear a jacket. They take appearances more seriously these days.'

We drive past school sports fields on the other side of the motorway. Redmond also points out the luxury accommodation that was – and still is – home to the wealthier students.

'How parents can stump up twenty thousand quid a year is a mystery to me. That's insane: no one should have to pay that much for education. On the other hand, it looks as if you get a lot for your money here. The pupils all appear wealthy these days; they have that self-assured walk. It's odd. In my time, I never thought of Marlborough as a place of privilege. It was more like a prison.'

How often could you go out?

'If there weren't any sporting activities, you could go out in the afternoons and at weekends. There were lessons on Saturday mornings, and after that you were free. I had a trusty three-speed Raleigh as a getaway vehicle. I would escape into the natural world, where everything seemed worthwhile.'

Did it make any difference to you that your parents only paid half fees?

'That wasn't something I really thought about at the time. It was only later that I realised that it set a kind of bizarre stigma on my forehead. The poor boys – and poor is of course a relative concept here – slept in dormitories in what were known as "in-college houses". The wealthier boys lived in "out-college houses", with servants and so on. Money was really the only difference: we all sat next to each other in the same classes and were on the same cricket team. Though they never came to our homes, and we never went to theirs. On the whole, the poor boys did best academically, while the rich ones were top in sports, being team captains and so on.

I only realised what a truly upper-class school looked like later, when I visited Winchester College. The teachers were of the highest calibre and the aim of sports was to enable pupils to focus better on their studies afterwards. There were readings in Latin during meals. When you got back from

Rudi Rotthier in front of the statue of Charles Darwin at the Oxford University Museum of Natural History

a match, you weren't allowed to drink until you had filled a silver beaker, which was attached to a silver chain, and first offered it to your best friend. What's more, the library possessed the original manuscript of Malory's *Morte d'Arthur*, which you could just leaf through, if you wanted to. I thought that showed real class.'

The memories of his school days bubble up.

'One of the older boys lent me a book that really fired my imagination: *The Private Life of the Rabbit* by R.M. Lockley. I was enchanted to discover that people were interested in reading about rabbits and that someone had taken the trouble to observe them and describe their lives in an interesting way.'

That was something you felt you could do too?

'It was something that seemed useful to me. To put my own experience of rabbits into words. Write stories about rabbits and thus make their lives, their biology comprehensible.'

But.

'I had set up a society, The God Society, whose aim was to refute the existence of God. We had invited the headmaster to give a talk to our members and he came, not having scrutinised our statutes, in the assumption that our aim was to *prove* the existence of God. He gave us that famous argument by William Paley. Suppose you were walking through a forest and you found a watch on the ground – would you assume that it had come into being by itself or that someone had made it? At the time people found it a convincing argument. I've heard my father use it too.'

What did the headmaster do when he found out that the society's aim was the opposite of what he had supposed?

'I don't think that he ever found out. We refuted God's existence to our own satisfaction and afterwards dissolved the society. Even then, I was using Darwin and evolution to back my arguments. Other boys raised the question of human suffering. Why would God create smallpox?'

You could also have cited inconsistencies in philosophy or in the Bible.

'We weren't that far at the time: we hadn't yet read the German theologians. The biblical arguments were later used against us, actually. When people witness the same event their accounts all differ. It would in fact be remarkable if everyone described things in exactly the same words, because it would look rehearsed.'

If it is inconsistent, it has to be true? That is a strange argument.

Redmond does not respond immediately. He is wool-gathering, lost in memories.

'Thank you,' he suddenly says.

What for?

'Thank you for our visit to the school.'

I assure him with my hand on my heart that I can take absolutely no credit for it.

'I couldn't have done it alone. The place is no longer bedevilled for me.'

He quickly waves the fragility of the moment away again.

'Not long ago I saw an advertisement for a dog that made me chuckle. "Labrador for sale. Eats everything, loves children." That kind of ambiguity appeals to me enormously.'

Then he is once more caught up in his thoughts for a while.

Chapter 4

FAMOUS FRIENDS

The time has come to speak of jealousy. For at least twenty years I have been untroubled by it; when it comes to the meanderings of human relationships I am inclined to tolerate or even welcome anything that falls – however remotely – under the mantle of love. But it assails me now as we sit expectantly on The Bell's terrace. The three of us are waiting for Colin, the dog that is allegedly destined to leap across our table at five o'clock, on his way to the green fields of freedom. The pangs that I am experiencing are not just because I no longer have exclusive possession of Redmond. They have to do with him retelling the stories that he told me to the unspecified journalist from The New Yorker. The journalist who is now also drinking Old Tripp.

I am the opposite of a storyteller. Once I have told an anecdote I have shot my bolt, and just telling it once is hard enough for me. But Redmond is able to repeat stories in more or less exactly the same precise, inventive words with undiminished pleasure and enthusiasm, as if he is thinking them up on the spot. And there was I thinking that he had spun them all just for me. Perhaps he prepares all his stories meticulously. Perhaps all those anecdotes about McEwan that he told me in the car were simply a rehearsal for this conversation. Perhaps he has told them all a million times before. Yet they sound spontaneous. Perhaps his spontaneity displays fixed patterns. At any rate, this feels like adultery.

What is even worse is that, in between the anecdotes, the man from *The New Yorker* asks more or less the same questions that I did. So much for originality. I muse gloomily on interchangeability, feel cosmically crushed. I am also struck by the realisation that Redmond ignores exactly the same questions when in full flow. It is a sign that he is engaged by a theme; the course of his narrative has already been mentally mapped out and he only responds fully to questions that help his story on. Others are answered, at best, with a monosyllable. 'Yes.' Sometimes, 'But'. Often there is no answer.

Answers come readily only if he does not have a topic in mind, or if he has said all he wants to say. In that respect, an interview is a war of attrition.

But we are cheered by the arrival of Colin, who does indeed leap onto the table, if not on the stroke of five, on his way to the nearby meadow to harry the local moles.

'I bet you thought I'd made it up. Look, he hasn't knocked over a single glass.'

Libby, one of the proprietors, claims that Redmond once suggested to a documentary maker, who thought that she looked good for an older person (Libby is, I think, in her thirties) that she should be in his documentary. 'I think the idea was that I would walk across this field. I was to disappear into the distance and be murdered.'

'It was only a suggestion,' Redmond reminds her, somewhat embarrassed.

The interviewer tries to bring the conversation back to the main topic, the writer Ian McEwan. Redmond ignores the first question and launches into his narrative.

'Ian's subject matter always relates to the place where he lives. When he moved to Oxford from South London, he lived in a flat above a cement courtyard. That resurfaced later in *The Cement Garden*. The house he describes in *Saturday* resembles the house in which he lives now.

His first wife, Penny, was a faith healer. She didn't much like Oxford. She said that so many of the people there, particularly the dons, had brown auras. Some were brown with purple spots, which is apparently a bad thing.

We went on a trip to Cornwall with Ian and Penny, and with Timothy Garton Ash and his wife Danuta. As a Catholic Pole, Danuta was susceptible to all that New Age stuff. Penny read her future in the cards and predicted that within twenty years, Timothy and Danuta's son would be jailed for serious assault. This revelation brought tears to Danuta's eyes.

Some of Penny's psychotherapist friends came to visit, and were lamenting for the umpteenth time the state of Oxford auras. I had remained silent throughout their conversation; suddenly one of the psychotherapists asked me what I thought. I said, "It's complete nonsense, bullshit from beginning to end. But I do think it's interesting to revisit the fifteenth-century mindset."

Ian defended her. He said, "Come on, Redsi, you know that we're all surrounded by an electromagnetic field." And we are, but you don't see it, and it's certainly not brown or purple.

A little while later, the conversation turned to Stonehenge. Somebody expressed wonderment at the fact that people were capable of moving such vast stones so long ago. Whereupon Penny replied, "Don't be so silly. Merlin sent them from Ireland." There was absolutely no doubt that she meant it; the wizard had pulled it off by mental power alone. I thought, poor Ian. But in a small voice that I had never heard before, and have never heard since, he said, "He sent them by Datapost." That was most courageous of him. She was highly dominant and had assumed that she would be able to go on dictating to him in intellectual matters, that she would be able to determine his reality.

When their break-up was nearing, her behaviour became increasingly erratic in a way that he found hard to interpret. At some stage he found out that she was constantly making telephone calls to the same number. It intrigued him, he rang the number himself, and discovered that it was an astrology helpline. He started ringing it every day. Overnight, Penny's behaviour became perfectly predictable: she was just following the advice that she was getting from the helpline.

His early books were full of her influence. *Black Dogs* marked a change, a new independence. With it, he moved away from her; it was his farewell to her world. From then onwards, truth and reason took on a central role in his writing and I think his fiction improved greatly as a result. I like to think that I had something to do with it, that I infected him with science. He started to read Darwin and Wallace avidly, then turned to works about physics, the Big Bang and that kind of thing. These days he knows much more than I do. He would read all the books that I sent to reviewers [when O'Hanlon was natural history editor of the *Times Literary Supplement*, RR]. Reading is an impressive business at his house. After dinner everyone withdraws with a glass of wine and reads for an hour or two, or even three. Not a word is said.

We went on some terrific hikes together, covering twenty or thirty miles at a time. Ian's disgustingly fit and extremely competitive; he sets off at the crack of dawn.'

All the talented writers of your generation seem to have known one another.

'We used to meet once a fortnight at James Fenton's house. At the time I wondered whether budding writers knew where to find one another at every university, but it turned out we were unusual. Julian Barnes was part of the group, as were the poets James Fenton and Craig Raine, Timothy Garton Ash, Martin Amis of course, Salman Rushdie, the philosopher Galen Strawson, Kazuo Ishiguro on occasion.'

No women?

'Ann Pasternak, Craig Raine's wife, was there sometimes.

I once took Bruce Chatwin to one of these gatherings, but he and James didn't get on. James leant back in his chair, put his feet on the table and shut his eyes. Bruce couldn't tolerate anyone falling asleep when he was holding forth. So he started talking more urgently, more dramatically. He did everything he could to attract Fenton's attention.' Redmond puts on a high, plaintive voice, '"When I visited Somerset Maugham, we were standing by the pond. He took me from behind and fucked me on the spot." Fenton opened a lazy eye. Then shut it again. Bruce ratcheted up the celebrity count. "When I visited Picasso's studio in Paris," or, "I always found Matisse such a pain." Fenton apparently continued to doze. I think that James, who prided himself on his connections and his skill as a raconteur, found it hard to be overshadowed. Chatwin never came back.

That is how Fenton expresses aggression; feet on the table and eyes shut. Ian simply falls silent.'

What did you talk about in the group? Sport? Football?

'Actually no. It is said that writers prefer to speak of anything but literature, but we were obsessed by books. I remember lengthy discussions about Nabokov, before I'd ever read anything of his, and about Saul Bellow.'

Did jealousy ever arise?

'Oddly enough I've never felt the slightest pang of jealousy. Bruce Chatwin would always say, "I'm not jealous of anybody. Probably because I'm so arrogant." Yet that was clearly a facade. I'm just happy that my friends are doing so well. Their value in the stock exchange of public esteem rises year by year. In that respect, I have made the best investment in friendship that you can imagine. In the old days, I would talk about my friend Ian and nobody knew who he was. Now when I mention him in a conversation I'm accused of name-dropping.

Fenton would sometimes say, "Redsi, why are you still hanging around here? Go home and bake a cake or do whatever it is that you're good at." That was the ethos: work hard and do something with your talent. Read, write reviews. Work on a book. We encouraged one other, read one another's work, gave one another the idea that what we were doing was really important. That's the stuff of true friendship.

It did help that everyone achieved a measure of success.

If jealousy ever did come into play it was between the two poets, Fenton and Craig. Craig once exclaimed at the ugliness of a pylon on Fenton's estate. James answered that he had looked into the matter and that it would cost a million pounds to remove the pylon. He went on to remark airily that he could afford to remove two pylons, which got Craig's back up. Craig had written the libretto for a Glyndebourne opera called The Electrification of the Soviet Union. With a title like that you can't expect a big hit, and it predictably folded after five nights. Fenton said to him, "If you want to make millions, you have to be ready and you have to be strong." Craig was completely convinced. He came to me and said, "Well, Redsi, I'm strong and, in a word, ready."

James is now so rich that it's ridiculous to be jealous of him.'

And what is the relationship between Ian McEwan and Martin Amis like?

'There is a certain rivalry between the two. Yet at the same time they hugely admire each other. You can feel them thinking, "What's he doing? I'd better apply myself and produce something really good." I think the reason they can remain such good friends is because they are very different as writers. They used to smoke a fair amount of dope. Both of them are so intense, so driven, so unbelievably fit. Dope calms them down slightly.'

'Which of McEwan's works do you admire most?' asks the man from *The New Yorker*.

Redmond finds it hard to select just one. He starts with *Atonement*.

'The intensity of McEwan's writing is extremely compelling. Knowing that his father had fought in the Second World War, I once suggested that he might try a novel on the subject. Strangely enough it's a conflict that has inspired relatively little literary fiction. When he was writing *On Chesil Beach*, he rang me up, wanting to know the name of a bird that sings at night. But it hadn't to be a nightingale. I asked him, "Ian, don't you know what's making that sound in the background?" A blackbird was singing outside.'

'What do you think is his least successful work?'

Redmond ignores the question and turns the subject to McEwan's ability to deal with criticism.

'If Craig criticises him, that's okay. But he can't stomach criticism from Martin; he finds it painful. I'm always amazed at how kind Ian is. If there are children in the house, they just wander into his study and it doesn't seem to bother him very much. He picks up the thread again without any difficulty.'

'Do you still meet regularly?'

'I used to think that the gatherings would go on forever. They did continue, albeit with reduced frequency – perhaps once a month – until we were in our fifties. Now they've stopped, though. The millionaires are busy. We are all too busy.'

And there have been some fallings out. For a long time, Barnes was not on speaking terms with Amis, after the latter had left his agent, Barnes' wife, for another literary agent, and Redmond and Galen Strawson don't get on any more either.

Redmond starts telling stories about travel writers: first, a meeting with the old explorer Wilfred Thesiger, when Redmond was working for the *Times Literary Supplement*.

'I wanted to publish excerpts from Thesiger's previous book. The great man himself opened the door. He showed me his library, which contained an extensive section on Arabia and many works about the Danakil who, he told me, cut off their poor neighbours' testicles. I asked him if we could take some photos. He took me to an adjacent room, containing an uncomfortable-looking camp bed from his soldiering days. He had a beautiful Leicaflex, with 30mm and 90mm lenses; near it lay a pile of photos. I picked one up. Thesiger was quick to object.' He puts on a grating voice, '"Not those, my dear." He didn't want the TLS to publish photos of boys or young men whom he found attractive. A little later he said, "I personally never encountered a single case of homosexuality among the Arabs." His Samburu boyfriend was in the house at the time of our meeting, but didn't put in an appearance.

Thesiger went on, "I was delighted that I could be of

service to the Danakil and other tribes. I had my instruments with me, my disinfectant, because when the youths become men ..." He mumbled something inaudible, then went on, "... circumcision. The skin is cut off on either side of the penis ... the incisions go right up the inner thighs. Of course, the youth must not scream. One scream and no woman will look at him ever again." He took pride in the fact that, wherever he went, he was placed in charge of circumcision.'

I recall Thesiger claiming that, with the exception of the bloodbath at Amritsar in 1919, the British Empire had been guilty of no serious wrongs.

'He must have known better. What about Tasmania, where the inhabitants were hunted like foxes? I think he saw the British as bringing peace, order and prosperity to the peoples they subjugated – a bit like the Roman Empire. He wanted to believe that the British Empire brought universal benefit. I think it was necessary for his peace of mind.'

This reminds him of a party at Pelican House to which he had invited the travel writer Norman Lewis.

'I reserved a room at a bed and breakfast for him and his wife. I booked an adjoining room, with a connecting door, for Martha Gellhorn. He was crazy about her, but they had never met.' He imitates Lewis's low, drawling tones, '"Awful B & B. But Martha Gellhorn was there, you know. If my long-suffering wife hadn't been with me, I might have broken down the door." When he arrived at the party, he said, "Who are these people? I don't know a soul. With your permission I shall take this lovely bottle, stretch myself full length upon the floor and get drunk." He drank like a fish. He once explained to me why there was a wire mesh around bottles of Rioja. "If you are working in the fields you can attach a piece of sacking to the metal lattice and pee on it. The pee evaporates and cools the wine."

You would never in a million years think that you were talking to a travel writer. Even when he was interviewing you, you wouldn't pay him any notice. When he was in a room, he was invisible. He possessed the gift of listening. In that respect he was the opposite of Bruce Chatwin, who always wanted to be the centre of attention. Chatwin always seemed to me more beautiful than a man had any right to be; at least, while he was still in good health. Lewis didn't interview people in the conventional way; instead he would tell them about himself.' He imitates Lewis once more, '"I have had four passions in life: cameras, fast cars, women and something else that I forget." I loved him. He seemed to write with such ease, though I'm sure that was deceptive. The first thing of his I read was *Voices of the Old Sea*. He was funny, but you never knew quite when he was joking, because he always adopted exactly the same tone. I can't remember that I ever saw him laugh. It wasn't something he did very often, though he always looked mischievous.'

'What do you think of Chatwin's books?'

'I loved *In Patagonia*. I read them all, but his short paragraphs got on my nerves. My favourite bit in *Songlines* is the passage about the old man, who wanted Bruce to stay in his smelly old caravan under a creaking gum tree. "Redders, I called him Hanlon in honour of you. He is a terrifying, rough man, who lives in squalor."

Chatwin said that in one respect – literary judgement – I was the most sensible person he knew, and he made me one of the executors of his literary estate. I thought he would soon change his mind, but he didn't. The other executors were Susannah Clapp and his wife, so I didn't actually need to do anything. But it was a great honour.'

The man from *The New Yorker* accompanies us as far as Pelican

House, where he intends to call a taxi. En route, we stop at a small supermarket. I put a one-pound coin in the trolley and we wheel it through the aisles. Redmond is enjoying himself. We buy stamps and breakfast cereals. Wine. A double supply of stamps, in fact, because 'if you stick on twice as many stamps, letters get there quicker'. We have already filled up the car with petrol, which means that today we have dealt with most of the points on this morning's list. Though we still haven't bought a roll of film. He asks me if I will keep track of the stamps. 'And remind me to post the letter first thing in the morning.'

The lady at the checkout has read *Trawler*. When it came out in paperback in the United States, the publisher rang to ask what he should do with the remaining hardbacks. Redmond, who was tipsy at the time, suggested he send the lot to Pelican House. An entire lorry load subsequently arrived. Since then, Annabelinda's customers have been given a signed copy of the book free with every purchase. The lady at the checkout also got a free copy.

'It's the only book in her house. It was a bit naughty, she thought.'

After a long wait the errant taxi arrives, and *The New Yorker* disappears out of our lives.

The chaos at Pelican House has not diminished in our absence. The cats have poked their noses in forbidden places. They have found the box of pralines that I had brought with me, have overturned it and opened it. They sniff and lick the pralines, but have not eaten any of them. The remains of the meal that the children prepared have grown mouldy. The miraculous proliferation of milk bottles has continued unabated. There are smells in the kitchen that I cannot immediately place, but that do not augur well. The dirty dishes cannot have increased in number, yet the pile seems higher. In these surroundings, habituation is a good thing. Once one has lost the habit of chaos, it is painful to return.

Redmond immediately switches on the washing machine.

Belinda rings; after a while Redmond passes her on to me. 'Cleanliness is very important to Redmond,' she says, without a trace of irony, referring to the washing machine, which he keeps forever running.

He drops in at the neighbours to ask their daughter to feed the cats, taking with him the binder with information about the beetle that has been named after him. 'You only appreciate the full significance of something like that when your neighbour is impressed,' he says afterwards. He has left the binder behind; the neighbour is to make copies. One more problem solved.

The fact that the neighbour's daughter is to be in the house over the next few days saddles us with a certain responsibility. We must make the place decent. We don't want her to take fright and call in the health and sanitary inspector.

'Piece of cake,' says Redmond, eyeing up the dirty crockery from afar. 'We'll get up really early tomorrow. Half past eight. We'll do some clearing up. It's not too bad. I mean, it's bad, but not that bad. Well, it's bad, but not disastrous. We'll get up, have some cereal, clear up, I will pack some clothes and we can be off again in a jiffy.'

Chapter 5

TO STONEHENGE

We are getting pretty attuned to one another. He lays the table, I make the coffee. We work our way through the cereal we bought yesterday. The box promises a breakfast high on vitamins and low on sugar, but despite lavish helpings of the never-ending milk supply, it tastes faintly of dust and glue. Afterwards I tackle the washing-up. Redmond fills a bin bag with anything that can be classified as smelly. He adds the glass or two that I break while washing up to the contents of his bag without reproach and goes off to fetch a pair of binoculars so that we can watch birds on our trip.

I am struck by how carefully he keeps Galen's room cat-free. During his argument with Belinda he pretended he wasn't prepared to; he answered back, but privately he cares. For the time being I respect his secret.

Time for a list.

Stick on stamps, I suggest, but Redmond has changed his mind. We will reach Belinda faster than the Royal Mail can, even with a double helping of stamps. Moreover, a fresh delivery of post (and milk) has arrived, which means we would have to buy yet more stamps.

So what should I write down?

'Film, at any rate.'

He gets into his stride. I try to keep up with his dictation. After eleven items he is out of breath. The final goal on our list is a journey to Dorset, place of Redmond's birth and – a few years ago – his mother's death.

By the time we have got through the morning's domestic programme and made the house presentable for the neighbour's daughter, it is time for lunch. We leave anyway. Although the first half of our itinerary takes us along the same route as the road to Calne a few days earlier, Redmond takes all the right turn-offs without hesitation.

Freud isn't troubling you today?

'My direction-finding ability is linked to my final destination.'

He has lost one of his hearing aids. This happened some time ago, but he mentions it only now. He may have lost it in the hotel in Calne, but it could have fallen out of his pocket somewhere else. That happens sometimes.

'Let's try and think where it could be.'

Shall I ring the hotel?

'Later. Then we'll try the other places we went to.'

And if no one has found it, shall we look in the car?

'Yes. That's a perfect plan. First, we'll look elsewhere, and if that doesn't help we'll search through the rubbish in the car.'

After we have applied ourselves to this task for a good half-hour he finds that we have been sufficiently industrious, and that we have earned a pint and a meal.

We end up on the terrace of the Swan Inn in Great Shefford.

A few ducks fly overhead. We are sitting beside a murmuring stream, with a view of shrubs and woodland. Redmond questions the proprietor about the birds to be seen in these parts. He is impressed by their variety.

He orders meat that he can only chew with difficulty, because of a dental plate.

'I can't remember any dreams from last night. I used to dream all the time, but now I seem to have lost the ability.'

Redmond is in therapy, and talks openly about it. Indeed, he is remarkably open about everything. He adores Helga, the Greek psychiatrist who has been treating him for over three years. It's something of a record for her – she has never before seen a client for more than a year. 'I'm quite proud of that. They say that Helga's in love with me, and find it unsavoury. She's read all my books, you know. I think she's enchanting.' He makes noisy kissing sounds, attracting the attention of two people at the table next to ours.

Initially he did not want to have therapy because he feared that tackling his demons might simultaneously jeopardise his ability to write. When, at the start of their sessions, he asked Helga, 'half jokingly' whether there was any danger that therapy would stifle his creative impulses, she did not laugh. '"That's quite possible," she said. "Psychiatric treatment is always dangerous for creative people." The aim is to make your highs less high and your lows less low. So you can't complain if that happens.'

In the end, though, he had no alternative. Belinda had told him that if he didn't go into therapy he would lose his family.

'Helga managed to reassure me. She told me that problems come in five or six categories and if you fall into one of them, you behave according to expectation. To me, it's reassuring that things are predictable, that your problems stick to the rules. I said to her, "I know you're a psychiatrist, but you're so wise.

Why don't you write Greek tragedies?" To which she drily replied, "My job is to avoid Greek tragedies." She's right, of course. It's quite an achievement for me to accept that prevention is better than description.

At first Belinda accompanied me to make sure I was honest. In the beginning I tried to maintain that everything was absolutely fine, that my wife had just got a bee in her bonnet that there was something wrong with me.

I had two recurring nightmares. It got to the point where I was frightened to go to sleep. In one of the two I would find myself travelling to a beautiful city. Sometimes it was Oxford, sometimes Siena or Rome. I would cross a square and find myself in front of a gigantic building with marble columns and flights of marble steps. In gold letters over the entrance it said ANNABELINDA. After an enormous struggle I would succeed in ascending the steps, where a uniformed porter would silently open the door. I would say, "I've come to see my wife. I'm her husband." He would answer, "I know who you are, but you're not welcome here." The door would shut again, leaving me standing at the top of the stairs, at a loss and without any money. In the middle of the square there was a little booth or kiosk of some kind. I needed to climb more stairs to reach the kiosk, but once inside it turned out to be a second-hand bookshop, with the intoxicating aroma of old volumes. But the books were in high bookcases, where I couldn't see them. There was a sign on the cases saying, "All first editions of Darwin priced at fifteen pence". Then I would wake up.

That dream tormented me emotionally. Helga asked me whether I ever saw Belinda's face during that dream. I told her I never did. Then she asked, "Why, do you think, is it so difficult for you to climb the stairs? And why can't you see the books?" I had no idea. Helga said, "Because you are a child. You are confusing your mother with your wife." What a humiliating and terrible realisation.

Since she told me that, the dream has never recurred. Before then I had had it perhaps three times a week, and when I woke up I was furious with Belinda. I asked her why she never wanted to see me. I acted as if she was responsible for her behaviour in the dream. She wasn't having any of it, which is hardly surprising. Now I see Helga less frequently.

In the other dream I would be returning from a long journey, for instance from the Congo, and was having difficulty finding my house. Somehow or other I would discover that Belinda had moved to the city, to a terraced house, because she wanted to live closer to Annabelinda. It was a terrible house, devoid of books. I would ask her, "Where are the books?" It would turn out that she had left them behind in our old house, but had forgotten to lock the door. In my dream I would drive around, trying to find Pelican House. Sometimes I would find it, sometimes I wouldn't. But even if I did, I was in for a nasty surprise. Everything had been left open, the door was rotten to the hinges and the books were mouldering on their shelves.

After this dream, too, I would wake up livid. I was increasingly angry, actually. Drinking, too, made me prone to fits of rage. I was so furious I couldn't control myself. Furious at Belinda – at least, that's what I thought.'

How did you get rid of the second dream?

'I can't remember, but again it was a case of conflating my mother with Belinda, whose face was never visible. Belinda loves literature whereas, apart from Dick Francis and that kind of thing, my mother hated books. She felt threatened by them. The vicarage housekeeper Rosiebud didn't like books either, but in her case it was because they attracted dust. Books meant more work for her. That I could understand.

When I was about eighteen or nineteen and a long-haired student of English literature at Oxford, my father arrived unannounced at the house I shared on Sunningwell Road with Douglas, my best friend, whom I had known since Marlborough College. Douglas was studying medicine.

My father told me he wanted to take me out to lunch at the Randolph Hotel, which was odd, as he had never done anything like that before. During lunch he lectured me, saying that from now on he intended to be a strict father and lay down the law. He insisted that we order a pudding. The meal lasted an eternity. At long last we got into his Ford Zodiac and returned to Sunningwell Road. When we arrived he sounded the horn and my mother emerged from the house. Without looking at me, she got into the car next to him. He turned round and accelerated out of the street with screeching tyres.

It was all very strange. I walked upstairs to my rooms to find them stripped bare of books. The only volume left was the collected poems of Wordsworth. I looked out of the window and saw a bonfire in the garden, where all my books were ablaze. The pictures my friends had painted for me had been added to this auto-da-fé. I ran downstairs in the hope of salvaging something, but she had emptied a jerry can of petrol over my possessions. The heat was overwhelming; I didn't manage to save anything.

Since then Wordsworth has been anathema to me. In my entire collection of books his was the one volume that they did not label "indecent and unsuitable". From that day on I have never set foot in the Randolph.

When my father rang the doorbell, my mother had been lurking in an alleyway. After we had gone off for lunch she had so terrified Douglas that he drove away in his car and didn't come back for ten days. He was useless, he didn't guard our house. When he came back, his first words were, "Is she still here?"'

He guffaws so loudly that a heron takes flight.

What possessed your parents to burn your books?

'I don't know. It's what Christians do, I believe. Burn books. Perhaps they had egged each other on. I think it's likely my father was behind the idea. Burning books would be more something for him.'

I take it you needed some of those books for your studies?

'Yes, but they didn't mind that as long as the indecent and unsuitable books – like Darwin's works – had been destroyed.'

After that incident you broke off all contact with home, I assume?

'No, I didn't, actually.'

Why not?

'I don't recall. I must have suppressed the memory. Oh yes: I needed their money. Unlike Belinda, I didn't have a grant. To evade tax, my father had made me the nominal owner of a caravan site that he possessed. I knew nothing about it, but on paper it meant that I had quite a decent income and therefore didn't qualify for a grant. He told me, "You cost me one pound a day." In those days that was a significant sum, more than I could earn myself.'

Tax evasion doesn't sound very Christian of a vicar.

'It was just plain dishonest.'

How terrible to have to go back because of the money.

'Afterwards I told my mother she had burnt a copy of a work that, despite bristling with devils, had once hung above an altar: The Garden of Earthly Delights by Hieronymus Bosch, a triptych that's now in Madrid. She wasn't impressed. "What kind of altar?" she asked. "Was it Roman Catholic?" I had to admit that it was. "Well then."

In her view, Roman Catholicism was practically as bad as atheism.'

The episode makes me think of exorcism, or the sort of treatment meted out to a member of a sect.

'It was a bit like that. I didn't go to church. I had long hair and friends they didn't like. I read books they despised. My father had written to the college chaplain, requesting that I be sent down so that I could be locked up. That plan did not succeed, so this was their alternative solution.

My parents' actions did convince me of something that has stayed with me ever since, namely that books really are important. They must be if they can upset someone to the extent that they're burnt on a cabbage patch. My father recently told me – not for the first time – that my books ought to be burnt.'

But you feel more hostile towards your mother than your father?

'Yes. Because she beat me as a child. She even beat me for crying. She beat me to teach me not to cry.'

He suddenly remembers that he does dream occasionally.

'These days I dream that I am travelling across country, on the way to a farm that I know well. Probably Belinda's farm. Foxes are at play and one of the foxes rubs his coat against my leg. I wake up and feel Bertie. That's a very happy dream.

It's strange, though, how a psychiatrist can get into your brain and draw out the poison. I used to wake up sweating, in a real panic. I often had difficulty remembering things, too. Helga says that the subconscious operates without words. She sits in her bare room and asks me questions. I tell her things, talk about my mother. And while I'm talking, all kinds of memories come back. I had forgotten a great deal until I went into therapy.'

He swallows a pill. He calls them caffeine or nicotine pills by turns, and has stopped offering them to me.

Redmond wants to show me Stonehenge. He used to go there as a child and nostalgically recalls a timeline that compares the genesis of the stone circle with contemporaneous events in ancient Egypt and Greece. 'With any luck we'll see a hippy or two.'

He has already related how the RAF planned to blast the monument to pieces during the Second World War, because it got in the way of a landing route, and that they used the spire of Salisbury Cathedral for target practice. 'In those days you couldn't really criticise the RAF. But the cathedral was taking things a bit far.'

For the second time, we drive through Hungerford.

He tells me about the Hungerford massacre. 'A member of a gun club abducted a woman, killed her and then went on a wild shooting spree. It must be about twenty years ago now. I think he killed fifteen or sixteen people before he eventually barricaded himself in a school. Police tried to negotiate with him, and somebody recorded the exchanges. The gunman said it was so easy to shoot other people, but rather harder to take his own life. Then there was a bang. It's so strange to think of it; people got shot just looking out of their windows to see what was going on. These days you have to leave your weapons at gun clubs; you can't take them home any more.

Look, a red kite.'

Are you sure it's not a crow pretending?

'Quite sure.'

At a crossing, he rubs his hands together. 'This is fantastic, a real adventure.'

How did you get the idea to travel, actually?

'James Fenton took me under his wing. I had just finished my doctoral thesis, which was on Darwin and Joseph Conrad and I didn't know what to do with my life. I didn't have much money. Fenton was younger than me, but he had travelled a great deal and was experienced. He had been a war correspondent in Vietnam, and it had left its mark on him. He was self-confident.'

And it was his idea to go to Borneo?

'Yes. I was an armchair traveller, content to read Conrad's accounts of regions like the Far East; I had never thought of actually going to those places and it certainly hadn't occurred to me that if you went far enough up river, you would find Dayak hunters who looked just like the ones in the earliest photos.'

What did Fenton want to do in Borneo?

'He wanted to snorkel and relax – to have a holiday, but in a jungle like the ones he'd seen in Vietnam. I thought, there's no story in that. As soon as I'd completed the SAS training course that was intended as preparation for our journey, I really wanted to go on an expedition.'

Was it the first time you'd been outside Europe?

'Yes. We stayed in a hotel in Kuching. Someone in the neighbourhood kept chickens and exotic birds; their cock crowed every morning. Cockfights were very popular; I suppose that explained the cock. But it reminded me of home, and I used to feel homesick as soon as I woke up. James gave me tips on how to get over it. He said, "When you arrive in a totally strange place, put your things in your hotel room, go out and by the time you come back, something extraordinary will have happened. By then you will regard your room as home and you'll think, everything is all right, I'm coming home." He was a very helpful guide in many respects, and it proved to be excellent advice. He cured my homesickness. I'd never been away from Belinda for any length of time since I'd been married, surprising as it may seem.'

So travelling didn't just happen; you had to be seduced into it.

'That's right. The most enjoyable bit, I quickly realised, consists of acquiring as many books as possible about the place that you intend to visit. You don't read in a remote, academic way; it's a much more intense, desperate business. You read in order to increase your chances of survival. That's an element of the whole business of travel that I still keep up. At the moment I'm reading everything that's been written about Spitsbergen.'

I do exactly the opposite. A place attracts my attention. I go there, and then I read about it – either during the journey or afterwards.

'I wouldn't like to say which is the best method. Once, when I was entering a village, I saw a pole with rotting meat tied to it. I concluded that it marked the birth of twins, having read that it is customary to hang up the placenta in such cases. But it could simply have been any old piece of meat hanging on a pole for some other reason.'

Why not just ask?

'That's a good question.'

We drive through military terrain. A roadside sign alerts us to the danger of Tanks Crossing.

'With a bit of luck we'll see tanks on an exercise.'

You might really have joined the army, then?

'For a while I was dead keen on the idea, and my parents thought I would. But when I found out that it involved following orders, I lost interest. That was not for me. Though it was really those chafing trousers that nipped my army career in the bud.

If they'd given us different kit for those drills at Marlborough, I might have been able to stomach the orders. You could really hurt yourself with those trousers.'

A second sign tells us that tanks have priority over other road users.

'You don't say. It's not hard to predict who'd come off worse in the event of a collision.'

So far there are no tanks to be seen, though we do pass a soldier on a bicycle.

'He's heading for one of those festivals where they recreate the First World War.'

Redmond's brain sizzles with possibilities.

'Or the army can't afford petrol anymore. Or all the tanks and motor vehicles are in Iraq and Afghanistan and the defence of the realm has been left to soldiers on bicycles.'

I guide him back to his first major journey. When you were in Borneo, did you immediately realise that this was your thing?

'I certainly did. The mere idea that you could earn money like that was intoxicating.'

Did you immediately find your style? Into the Heart of Borneo is rather a different piece of writing from your thesis.

'Yes. I found it most liberating after years of turning out academic prose.'

Did you ever find it difficult to write about yourself?

'No, because I see myself as a character in the plot.'

But that character is the real you?

'Yes and no. Before I leave, I plan the book like a novel, but my main characters run away with the story, the bastards.

Borneo was a short trip, barely two months. The book had to be a comic one for the simple reason that we didn't have much material. At first, James didn't want me to write about him at all. He only agreed because the book was to be published by his brother Tom, who ran a struggling garage press by the name of Salamander. There was no publicity budget; the book owed its success mainly to word of mouth advertising. Not long afterwards Salamander Press found itself on the brink of bankruptcy. Its bookkeepers were unfazed and said, "Just publish another book like the one on Borneo."

The book was finished within a year, which is extremely rapid by my standards. The South American journey that inspired my next book lasted four months; the writing took about two years. In the case of the Congo, the journey lasted six months and the writing took seven years.'

Why did writing become such a struggle?

'Well, the Congo book was always going to be the magnum opus. I had that in my head right from the start. That was Conrad country and I didn't want to go there too soon. So I first went to two other major jungle regions in preparation for the Congo.

The Congo journey was of an entirely different nature. It was much more disconcerting; there was a lot of sorcery. It was peculiar to see how everyone depended on their own personal fetishes. I sometimes felt that in that place, the subconscious had been made visible for all to see. There was a fascinating sense of how everything had indeed begun there, or at least in Africa. It was hard to find the right register when I was writing about it.'

How does someone who sets great store by reason write about magic?

'The role of sorcery was so powerful that you couldn't deny it.'

You couldn't accept the magic, but at the same time you couldn't get away from it?

'Exactly.'

What makes jungles so attractive?

'The wonderful feeling that the unknown lurks around every corner. Jungles are such treasure troves of animal and plant life. I was reminded of the eggshell that fell at my feet on the vicarage lawn. You feel like a child, everything is new, you've no idea what's going on. You're scared, you've got a damp crotch the whole time. Your canoe rounds a bend and you see an animal that you can't immediately place – is it a bat, a bird or a butterfly? When it flies over you get a good look, though, and it turns out to be a butterfly with black, wicker-work-like markings. It's exciting. The world looks fresh and new. The jungle is wonderfully chaotic; it's a place that you can never master, never fathom.'

Chaos attracts you.

'Yes.'

I can't imagine writing for seven years about a journey that took six months, I tell him. That sounds like torture to me. Ideally, I journey for longer than I write. I enjoy writing, but travelling is so much more fun.

'There was another project in the offing, a journey to the jungle of New Guinea, to the hidden plateau that was in the news a few years ago, in 2006 I think, when new species were found there. But my daughter was ill, I didn't want to go. By spending so long on *Congo Journey* I effectively prevented myself from going. And now I'm too old for a jungle trip, I think. It's such an effort. I would be a hindrance to my companions, would endanger them.'

About six miles outside Stonehenge the traffic slows, we drive at a snail's pace, then grind to a halt in a traffic jam.

Are all these people on their way to Stonehenge?

'I sometimes picture a skeleton behind the steering wheel

of each car. A skull and bones. I don't like imagining that, but the image pops up in my mind. It's not very constructive to think along such lines.'

The traffic jam comes to an end, as do the dark thoughts.

'Good heavens, there it is! How absurd that the road runs just past it.'

A lonely hippy, sitting in a deckchair beneath a sign bearing the legend FREE THE STONES, is selling stickers, collecting signatures and, when called upon, explaining her manifesto. We walk past her.

The circle of stones is smaller than Redmond remembers them. 'Whereas in the case of Avebury they seemed bigger.' The timeline that he was so enthusiastic about as a child has gone, presumably rendered obsolete by new theories and discoveries. A path has been created. Many visitors follow an audio tour, guided by little electronic devices. Others sit on the grass, canoodling, playing guitars and generally enjoying themselves.

Redmond is fascinated by the flocks of birds. 'Odd how many starlings there are. And there's a jackdaw. Jackdaws like sea cliffs and church towers. It makes sense that they feel at home here. But starlings and cliffs don't go together at all. What are they doing here? Look, there – a peregrine falcon. And a kite. What a lot of birds. In the Congo you would just accept that they were the spirits of the dead.'

We encounter a group of Japanese people photographing a sheep.

'Don't they have any sheep in Japan?'

Redmond doesn't seem to mind the hordes of tourists with their headsets and guiding devices. 'I like to think that one of them will retain an interest in this place and perhaps research its origins. I know that there are all kinds of different theories about Stonehenge, but it's hard not to regard it as a religious centre. The Mecca of its day. Or perhaps the Woodstock. A place people came to from near and far – that people still come to from near and far. Look, a lark.'

Every few minutes he spots another species.

'More starlings. Starlings are also good at imitating other birds.'

He buys rolls of film in the Stonehenge souvenir shop. We do not post the letters. He does not take any photos.

Chapter 6

WILD PONIES

Redmond drives into Salisbury and parks outside a super-market. We follow a scenic route into the centre, alongside a small river, down pedestrian-friendly streets. One of the buildings that catches our eye is a pub called The Mill, that we will undoubtedly visit later.

Shall we just go there straight away?

But Redmond's objective lies elsewhere for the time being. The cathedral and, before that, the bookshop. Beach's Bookshop, which is no longer there. On the site where it once stood is an Italian restaurant that is part of the Prezzo chain.

What was so important about the bookshop that it warrants a visit even though it no longer exists?

'It was run by two old spinsters. They seemed to me to be about a hundred and twenty years old, whereas they were probably about fifty, if that. I think they're still alive somewhere in a nursing home. That seems to be the deal for women: if they renounce men, they cease to age, they achieve immortality. For men, the opposite is true: without women they can't survive.'

Why was the bookshop so special, though?

'You could get eclairs across the road.'

That is pretty special. The sight of the restaurant appears to pain Redmond.

'Let's move on for now. That's where Edward Heath used to live after he was Prime Minister.

Besides being a parish priest, my father was also a canon and every now and then, perhaps once a month, he used to go to the Chapter House in Salisbury to meet the Bishop. During the holidays I would go with him. While he was in his meeting the old spinsters were happy to let me hang around the bookshop. I was just tall enough to see over the counter; I must have been about ten. What I wanted above all else was Morris's *British Birds* [Rev. F.O. Morris, *A History of British Birds*, published in the mid-nineteenth century, RR], with its beautiful, hand-coloured illustrations. If I remember rightly, the whole set cost two pounds and sixpence. (These days it fetches around six or seven hundred pounds.) My pocket money didn't stretch to such a sum, so I offered the ladies what I had, which was ten shillings, and they gave me the first volume. Each time I gave them all the money I possessed, and once it reached the necessary amount, I was given another volume. They kept the rest of the set back for me. The fact I had to wait so long for it made each volume even more special.

It was heavenly being in the bookshop. When my father came back, an hour or two later, he must have thought that I had been bored, but nothing could have been further from the truth. I hadn't even exhausted the delights of the natural history section. I examined every book. They smelt divine. Each had lovely illustrations, and the loveliest of all were in the book that I was buying by degrees. After these browsings I would go off with my father, to be unsettled by the way in which the natural world echoed the printed page. Whenever I encountered a bird looking exactly like its picture and description in books, a strange kind of shock would go through me. That kingfisher must have read the same book, I would think, and decided to dress up like its picture. It took a surprisingly long time – years, in fact – before I realised that I'd got things the wrong way round. For me, the fact that birds in nature looked like the illustrations in my books was nothing short of a miracle.'

We approach the cathedral. Redmond points out the Bishop's Palace where he once ate strawberries and cream in the Bishop's garden.

All you could eat?

'No, you got one helping and that was it.'

He points to the spire. 'Spitfires used it for target practice during the war, you know.'

We cross a lawn and enter the cathedral.

What most impressed you when you came here as a child?

'This very spot, in fact. These same magnificent cloisters. The idea of wandering around here and thinking great thoughts appealed to me. I felt that you would automatically think great thoughts if you spent a lot of time here. I didn't even know what great thoughts were, but I was sure I would have them one day.'

Each canon had a seat near the bishop in the cathedral stalls. Redmond wants to find his father's seat. On the way, his attention is diverted.

'Clock-spotters come from all over the place to see this. It's the oldest working clock in the world.'

A sign states that it dates from 1386.

'Ha! Just in case you didn't believe me.' He points to a rusty, pointed bit of metal. 'Here's the tip of the cathedral spire, complete with bullet holes courtesy of the RAF. They replaced it in 1950.'

We find the canons' stalls. I'd expected to see his father's name on the seat, but it only gives his parish: Calne.

'I remember the Bishop's shoes. He was dressed in purple, but from my low-level perspective as a child I could see that he sported crocodile-skin boots.'

Redmond looks up from the stalls, taking in the vaults and stained-glass windows. 'No wonder my father found it easy to believe in God in such glorious surroundings – a gorgeously sculpted and gilded cocoon of privilege. It would have been trickier for him elsewhere.'

Did you experience religious feelings here too?

'At first. That's the whole point of a building like this. It's designed to overwhelm you. A kind of divine putsch.'

Were you an altar boy?

'We didn't have altar boys. But I was in the choir, like my brother.'

You sang like an angel?

'Not really.'

We pass the stone figures of knights lying on top of tombs, their feet supported by little dogs.

'Those figures spoke to me as a child; they expressed a sentiment I could understand. I realised that those long-dead people, too, loved their dogs. However remote their lives were from mine, that was something I shared with them. Now let's make tracks for The Mill.'

How did your parents actually hit upon the name Redmond? I put the question as we retrace our steps past the late bookshop.

'My ancestors, the O'Hanlons, came from Northern Ireland

originally. They had a castle in Tandragee. We went there when I was about eight, because the castle came up for sale. I remember a gigantic staircase and tapestries on the walls. My family managed to scrape together three thousand pounds, but it wasn't enough.

Many years later, at a dinner being given for the head of ITV, I found myself next to Lady Longford. She asked me, "Are you an O'Hanlon of Tandragee? My dear, our estates abut." Whereupon I, feigning distraction, said something like "Oh really?" As if I had so much land that I couldn't possibly be expected to know what it bordered on. She asked, "Have you been back to your ancestral home?" "Not since I was a child." "Well, my dear, I have bad news for you. Your castle has been turned into a potato-crisp factory." She uttered the last three words with exaggerated jaw movements, a bit like Popeye in animated films.

To be honest, I don't think the current castle bears much relationship to the place my forebears lived in, which I suspect was no more than a keep with loopholes. It was later extended by the Dukes of Manchester, after Oliver Cromwell installed them there.

I was named after Redmond O'Hanlon, a seventeenth-century rapparee who fought against Cromwell with his little army. A rapparee was a cross between a guerrilla fighter and a gangster. His army would not have numbered much more than about ten horsemen. All Catholics, of course. Redmond was a hero of the resistance and caused so much trouble that a price was put on his head. His cash-strapped brother cut his throat while he was asleep, chopped off his head, stuck it on a pike and bore it to the leader of Cromwell's garrison. That was very Irish. His own brother had killed him for money, but the family could maintain that Redmond had never been vanquished by

Cromwell. So in a sense everybody won. Redmond acquired a reputation, his brother gained financially. That didn't make Redmond any less dead, of course. The O'Hanlons were Celtic lords who carried the banner of the King of Ulster. They had subjects who paid tax; in return they offered protection. But they could do little against a regular army like Cromwell's.'

Isn't it strange that your Anglican father gave you the name of a Catholic hero?

'I never thought about it in that light.

Anyone who crossed the water and ended up in England or Scotland was well advised to convert. You would never find work as a Catholic. Most of the O'Hanlons gave up the O in their names; they became Hanlons and anglicised completely. While my ancestors at least kept their O, they went overboard in converting to the most extreme form of Protestantism. My grandfather married a Sloane, a truly fundamentalist family from the Glasgow area. They owned a fleet of steamships that transported coal from Aberdeen. Passengers could travel on them too, but it was no picnic; the ships were small and rolled about, and by the time you disembarked you were black with coal dust. On a recent trip to the Outer Hebrides, I mentioned that my grandparents owned steamships, and was surprised when the older people started to chuckle with pleasure. They had fond memories of those awful vessels.'

Speaking of ships, your father's decision to marry an actress must have rocked the boat, coming from a background like his.

'Yes. At the time my grandfather was a billionaire, with seventeen full-time house staff. He had made his money in velvet, with textile factories in Manchester and Belfast. His firm supplied great names such as the actress Sarah Bernhardt, but his big break came with the wars. The First World War brought Zeppelin raids, the Second World War attacks by German bombers, and during both conflicts people were ordered to hang thick blackout curtains in their windows to thwart the enemy. Heavy O'Hanlon velvet proved popular for this purpose.

My grandparents and their horde of domestic servants lived in a grand mansion. My grandfather would follow my mother as she tripped about this huge house, going down on his knees in his fine suit to wipe away her footprints with a silk handkerchief. I take it that was his way of symbolically purging his home of malign female influence – that's the kind of religious extremist he was. Later she left her shoes at the door and walked around on her stocking feet. I don't know if he regarded that as an improvement.'

So your father had defied his parents?

'Yes. He rebelled against his fundamentalist origins by becoming an Anglican priest and marrying an actress. But he couldn't really rid himself of his early influences.

My grandfather had another side to him. During the Second World War, families were evacuated from London to the countryside, where they were safer from the bombings. If they were lucky, these urban refugees might be picked up in a modest family car. But the woman and children allocated to my grandfather found a Rolls-Royce waiting for them, with a uniformed chauffeur. They took this as a sign that they would be well fed. Indeed, they were, but they had to say their prayers first.

The house has now been converted into an old people's home.'

What happened to his fortune?

'It disappeared, eaten up by taxes. The various family members distrusted one another, and they were more inclined to splash their money around than pool it. They built country residences in the Lake District. The crisis of 1929 hit them hard, with pretty appalling consequences, I think, in some cases.

My mother, by contrast, came from a family of medical officers who were careful to live within their means. My parents kept their money separate. I don't know why; I think my mother paid for everything.'

As we drive out of Salisbury, Redmond points to a nunnery.

'We came here from Marlborough College on a retreat. I took my group to the pub, where we smoked Players. They tasted awful and made me feel sick; it was before the days of filter-tipped cigarettes. When we returned, the front door was locked. We discovered an open window at the rear of the building, through which we climbed, to find ourselves in a nun's bedroom. The noise woke her up. I apologised and explained our position as honestly as possible. Whereupon she simply said, "God bless you my son." She didn't tell on us.'

Although the sun is already setting, Redmond is determined to reach Dorset. 'The road past the hills is more scenic, but if we follow this route we can take the ferry – indeed, have to take it – which to me is an exhilarating prospect. I still feel as excited as a child at the prospect of a ferry trip. Even when it's only a short crossing, it's always a bit like going abroad. As soon as we're on the boat I feel as if I'm on holiday.'

That is a pleasure yet to come. First we pass the site of another memory. It is a village called Coombe Bissett and Redmond does not want to stop there. He points out the church and the vicarage.

'My father came here after he had had a mental breakdown in Calne. We had to look after him for about a month, I think, because my mother had gone on a ridiculous mission to Poland, where she presumably hoped to convert Roman Catholics. Belinda looked after him, actually, because I was writing my thesis on Thomas Hardy.'

So he suffered from depression too?

'Yes. I remember realising at the time that depression is not the same thing as melancholy. He was racked by terrible fears and the torments that he experienced left him bathed in sweat.'

Redmond assumes that his father experienced a crisis of faith in the margins of that depression, but is not sure.

'People can be seriously disillusioned by God after allowing their whole lives to be governed by His nonsense, taking the wrong decisions, hating or being hated in His name. Perhaps my father became aware that his hate was based on a lie. At that stage of his life he was, of course, too old to start afresh, being by then in his fifties. He lamented that he had not gone into the family business.

Later he was admitted to a London hospital, where he received electric shock treatment. The idea behind it is that the brain consists of a series of electric circuits and that by applying severe shocks you can alter their dynamics. It causes powerful seizures and patients have to be strapped down to prevent them from breaking their legs. Somehow or other it must have worked, because for a long time after that he was all right again. He continued to be given this treatment at intervals, though I was not told at the time. The subject was never brought up, because it was too awful to contemplate.'

It sounds like *One Flew Over the Cuckoo's Nest*.

'Absolutely. Towards the end of his life, my grandfather went into an institution in Bournemouth, where he was to stay for thirteen years. Again, I was kept in the dark. My grandmother didn't visit him and nobody mentioned his name, because losing your faith or becoming depressed was regarded as a sign of God's displeasure. There was no good reason for a billionaire to become depressed. Or for my father. Or for me. It just happens out of the blue. The family scourge poses a risk to Galen and Puffin; my brother seems to have escaped.'

In the Roman Catholic Church, priests can at least let off steam by indulging in the pleasures of the table, or the bottle. Or turn to other carnal joys that are less officially tolerated. Did your father have some way of relieving his feelings?

'He didn't drink very much. When times were good he found release in sailing. He used to take part in competitions in Poole Harbour. Come to think of it, that's the only time I ever heard him swear. He got out of position at the start of the race and said, "Damn." Followed by, "Good heavens." But he didn't raise his voice, just said it in his usual mumble.

Shortly after I left Marlborough College, one of the better sailors found himself in need of crew, so took me along with him. I didn't have to do anything really, other than redistribute my weight occasionally, and we finished second in the national championship. We made a fine picture, too, what with the wind in our hair and water flying all over the place; the girls loved it. Whenever we overtook my father – which happened a couple of times – I waved enthusiastically. That wasn't appreciated.'

It doesn't really sound as if sailing was a relaxing pastime for him.

'No, and he was always the butt of jokes. You know the kind of thing: I see you came in last, canon, God must have been having forty winks, eh? Though he did occasionally win something.'

Did your father and mother love one another?

'She used to say, "It's a good job he's a vicar, because if he leaves me in the lurch, he'll get the sack." I don't think there was ever the slightest chance that he would have left her or fallen for someone else. She was very domineering.'

Was she interested in other men?

'No. There was once a television series in which a woman didn't want to have sex with her husband, whereupon he raped her. My father had slipped away from dinner and was caught watching this scene.' Redmond imitates his mother's shrill voice, '"Douglas!"'

He fishes once again in his pockets and digs out a caffeine or nicotine pill. He has talked non-stop for seven or eight hours, acted as tour guide, driven the car. I am exhausted from listening, sitting and following.

We drive through the geography of his memory. The chronology is not always clear to me; we cross the time zones of his life in all directions, but there can be no doubt about the geography.

How long is it till we get to Dorset?

'A couple of hours. It depends on the ferry.'

Shouldn't we take a break?

'Do you think so? I can easily carry on driving.'

Let's have a break.

Somewhere he has spotted a bed-and-breakfast sign and we take a left turn. At a T-junction we turn right. We drive mile after mile, but see no bed and breakfast anywhere.

We do see a lot of other things though: wild ponies, donkeys and prehistoric cattle, and Redmond assures me of the presence of pigs. 'They provide a great eco-balance by eating acorns, which are harmful to ponies. That used to be cited as evidence of the workings of Providence: the acorns fall, the pigs eat them and grow fat, at the same time protecting the horses for whom acorns are poisonous, and as winter approaches, you slaughter your pig, add salt and end up with ham. The Lord's goodness in a single flowing equation. As a child, I used to wonder why He had hidden salt away so well. I never quite knew where the ancient Britons got their salt.'

A young donkey sprawls stubbornly across the road, forcing the traffic off the tarmac.

'That's the New Forest for you,' says Redmond, pleased by the donkey's obstruction.

The forest's name is misleading. The heathland was declared part of the royal hunting domain at the time of William the Conqueror.

'The ponies aren't truly wild. Every now and again they are rounded up and branded. I don't think that we are heading in the right direction for the B&B. We should have gone left at the turning.' He turns the car round and we indeed find Gorley Tea Rooms, the signposted bed and breakfast, just past the turning. It stands opposite a pond whose waters twinkle in the evening light.

While Redmond parks the car, I enquire whether they have any rooms for us. A receptionist who is clearly new and previously employed at Fawlty Towers allocates me two rooms and has me pay for them, only to discover that they are not in fact available and that she cannot refund the money I have transferred through my credit card. 'Why do credit card companies make transactions so complicated?' She gets in a bit of a state, but eventually finds us a double room that can be partitioned and goes in search of some cash to refund the difference. Redmond, who has meanwhile joined me, watches her with an amused expression. 'A plunging neckline and a short skirt – that helps with the tips. My daughter Puffin works in a restaurant and she says that people tip her in inverse proportion to the length of her skirt. As you can imagine, this scientific finding had an effect on her hemlines.'

The receptionist has managed to find some money somewhere and shows us to the room, where Redmond immediately installs himself in the cramped annex. He does so in the way that James Fenton taught him: by hurling down his

Redmond's daughter Puffin

luggage with careless abandon. We argue briefly about where each of us will sleep. There is no earthly reason why I should have the larger bed and the larger room.

'Yes there is,' says Redmond emphatically. 'I always go to sleep immediately after dinner. You might want to do some more work, or read or watch television.'

There is also another, unspoken, reason. He is looking after me. His concern for my comfort has been something of a leitmotif on this trip. He doesn't lay it on too thick, but there is no budging him now. He invokes his craving for sleep.

'You know, I've always depended on mechanical alarm clocks, but they just don't meet my needs. I need an alarm clock that only goes off after fourteen or fifteen hours, whereas with mechanical ones, the limit is twelve hours. After twelve hours of sleep I'm only just getting into the swing of oblivion. Since you sleep less, you must have the bigger room.'

Another problem arises, though. In Redmond's annex there is a little window that overlooks the pond and the ponies. But the window is locked. The combination of small room and lack of ventilation troubles him. Once again, I offer to swap. 'We could leave the dividing door open and open the window on your side.' That window overlooks the car park, not the pond and the ponies.

I go to the receptionist and ask for the key to open the other window. My request rattles her; she progresses from a bit of a state to full-blown panic. She comes in person, gesticulating nervously, to establish that the window is indeed locked. After scouring the drawers industriously for keys, she rings for help. 'I'll bring the key to you as soon as possible.' A quarter of an hour later she comes back to explain matters. 'I'm afraid you're not going to be able to unlock the window. I can't find the key, but even if I could, I wouldn't be allowed to give it to you.'

Why not?

'The windows on that side mustn't be opened, because that would endanger the ponies.'

The ponies?

'Yes. They might stick their heads through the windows and get stuck. We can't take the risk.'

What if we just open the window very slightly – a mere crack – so that not even the tiniest pony could possibly stick its nose through it?

'It's not allowed. And it's impossible, because I haven't

got the key.' It seems we must wrestle not only with a closed window, but also with faulty logic. It is impossible and it is not allowed. Or the other way round.

We just leave the dividing door open.

'Later,' says Redmond, 'we must find out how many ponies get injured every year by sticking their heads through windows. Now there's a useful object for study.'

Next door to the Gorley Tea Rooms is a pub, the Royal Oak, where I order curry (which according to Redmond has now displaced fish and chips as the national dish) while he opts for a faggot (a word, he tells me, one has to be careful with). There is also live music on the menu, provided by a local band called Axel and the Whales. They play reasonably proficient jazz rock and make no attempt to dress up their act in any way. The lead singer, whom I take to be Axel, occasionally addresses his sparse audience in an American accent. A fake one, according to Redmond. A regular at the bar, with whom he got chatting, has assured him that Axel only talks American when he's performing. 'He was born in the neighbouring parish. He's as local as the ponies.'

We find it hard to talk above the music. Redmond revels in the details, savouring the way in which the saxophonist carefully lines up two and a half pints for the first part of the performance. 'That'll get me through a few numbers,' he calls out, waggling his eyebrows up and down. 'You mustn't lose sight of the essential things in life.'

Many of the customers are from out of town. When we ask if she is a local, the waitress answers with an emphatic negative. It turns out that she was born four miles away.

'In the countryside, the world is very small indeed,' says Redmond. 'One grain of sand is not like another.'

In between two numbers he points out that there is also a contradictory phenomenon. 'I once spent a few months on the Orkneys, on one of its tiny northernmost islands. While I was there, it seemed to me as if the island grew in size. I got to know more and more people. Over time, the grain of sand grew to become a world.'

Chapter 7

BIRDWATCHING

'Well,' says Redmond, somewhat crestfallen. 'You never know what's going to happen on this trip.'

The ferry, which he has been looking forward to for several days, is not running. The boat normally takes holidaymakers and commuters between Bournemouth and Studland, across Poole Harbour, saving them a journey of fifteen miles or so by road. Why weren't there signs several miles back that the ferry wasn't running? And why isn't the ferry running?

Harry, a pensioner lugging a pair of formidable binoculars, answers our second question. Part of the slipway had started to crumble away, and the ferry operators didn't want to risk an accident. So for the next ten days or so crossings have been cancelled while repairs are carried out. Meanwhile another, larger ferry passes, shuttling between Poole and Cherbourg.

'You could just drive there,' Harry suggests. We linger for a while, absorbed by the spectacle of the repair work. Redmond's attention shifts to Harry, who is having the time of his life on a sunny day, drinking in the activity around him, entranced by every boat and every bird, while his wife waits in the car, counting the minutes until they leave.

' A scene of everyday tolerance. A family outing on a Saturday morning.'

Whereas we are on an expedition.

'Exactly.'

Our expedition now faces a considerable detour. According to Redmond, Poole Harbour is the largest natural harbour in Europe, though it has the drawback of being rather too shallow. Dredgers are at work, carving out a deeper channel for larger, seagoing vessels. Once on the road again, we drive past Parkstone. 'Belinda and I lived here for a while, in a house that my mother had inherited from a former teacher, an old spinster who taught English and drama. My mother was her favourite pupil. It was one of a row of virtually identical terraced houses, each with a little garden; a dead end sort of place.

During that time I helped someone move to Exeter and with the money I made I bought an art book of work by Georg Grosz. Belinda wasn't too pleased; we were hard up and the whole point of the job had been to make a bit of extra cash. Instead I came back with less than I started off with.'

Did your parents like Belinda?

'They did, despite her being an atheist – worse, a lapsed Catholic. My mother was in the habit of saying, "Once a Catholic, always a Catholic." She talked some incredible nonsense.'

Though there does seem to be a difference between people from Catholic countries and people from countries with a Protestant ethos.

'Yes, people from Catholic countries are much nicer.'

The journey does not go without a hitch. Dorset, like the rest of rural England, is peculiarly short on road signs, as if it is assumed that anyone using the roads already knows the way. Redmond is also nonplussed by the changes that have taken place over the last forty years.

'There never used to be any roundabouts here before,' he complains, whenever one of these offending structures causes us to take a wrong turning.

He starts to tell me about the Saxon church at Wareham, the next little town, 'the oldest church in the country, I believe – not that there's much to see, but it's still in use.' Before we get to Wareham, however, we have to halt by the side of the road. An endless stream of Harley-Davidsons, preceded by a police motorcycle escort, approaches from the opposite direction.

'Incredible. All those old men.'

There must be at least a hundred of them.

'And they all look at least a hundred years old.'

Some of them bear Union Jacks. They have grey beards.

'Look at those bandannas. They think they're Peter Fonda. That's what's behind all this. *Easy Rider* came out when they were young and impressionable. Now they're all lawyers and bank managers, or retired, but for a glorious moment they're managing to forget that and are playing at being tough guys. Something tells me that the current economic crisis poses no immediate threat to Harley-Davidson. In half an hour's time they'll stop to have a pee – at their age you have to do that quite often, as I know to my cost – after which they'll order half a pint of beer. A pint would be too risky. Then they'll go back home. Some have long hair, but I see none of them have tattoos. Life on the wild side.

Most of them drive Harley-Davidsons, but you also see the odd Enfield or Triumph. A bike like that costs around £5,000, which puts them out of reach of teenage rebels. Motorcycling is actually pretty dangerous, though I read somewhere that seventy per cent of accidents happen not to youths on their Suzukis, but to old geezers driving too slowly and tipping over.'

The procession includes a van bearing the legend 'Lord's Taverners'.

Who are these heavenly innkeepers?

'No idea. But things have come to a pretty pass if there's such a thing as motorcyclists for God. Good grief. We must be up to the two hundred mark by now. What a glorious noise they make. A shame, though, that English manufacturers are so under-represented.'

I make it three hundred motorcycles.

'At least.'

At length a police Land Rover marks the end of the convoy and the traffic is permitted to move on again.

'Well, we might not be in the Congo, but there's plenty going on. There'll be a carnival in Wareham tomorrow.'

You don't say. What does that involve?

'They'll choose a Miss. There'll be a parade. And the best or most spectacular vegetables will get an award.'

That is indeed nearly as good as the Congo.

'Colin Thubron and I often give lectures together. Someone once asked him whether he might consider writing a travel book about his own country. He said that was quite out of the question. There are already far too many travel writers who owe their reputation to books on exotic places that nobody's ever heard of – they later return from these far-flung locations in broken health and are reduced to writing about their own country, thus losing whatever small measure of credibility they possessed. That preyed on my mind when I was travelling around the north and in the Orkneys. In a sense it paralysed me.

Here's the Saxon church. Small, but with quite a high tower and built of stone, which must have been impressive at the time. Fifteen hundred years ago this was a trading centre, but the harbour has silted up since then.'

He savours the place names. 'This river is called the Piddle. The other is the Frome. We're now on the Dorset heath, which has its own ecosystem; it can't be used for farming.'

Speaking of ecosystems, why did you decide to grow side whiskers?

'Out of affection for Darwin and Huxley. I thought that if I looked like T.H. Huxley I would be able to write as well as he did. During my time at Oxford I used to go to lectures by the literary critic John Bayley which were all the more impressive because he stammered. He always had a Meerschaum pipe; a lovely yellow thing. For many years after that I used to smoke a similar pipe, which I filled with exactly the same brand of tobacco that he used. Clan pipe tobacco from the Netherlands.' Redmond looks at me dubiously. 'Or it might have been Belgium.'

Why did you stop?

'Belinda didn't like it. She loathes the smell of tobacco.'

He points to the ruins of Corfe Castle on a nearby hilltop.

'At the time of the Civil War, this was a Cavalier stronghold. But it had been built during the days of bows and arrows and boiling pitch. Cromwell ranged his cannons against it and blew its walls to rubble. The castle was never completely rebuilt.'

It is a dramatic ruin of the kind you see on paintings.

'A romantic spot by full moon. An English king was murdered there. They wanted to do it in a way that wouldn't leave any marks, so they stuck a red hot poker up his anus, to make it look as if he had died a natural death. My mother would tell me this story, milking it for its full horror value. She loved anything that she could dramatise. She would describe the king's murderers creeping in through a door hidden in a wall panel and killing him. As a child I would anxiously tap the walls of my bedroom to make sure that there were no secret panels in them.'

Were you frightened they'd get you with a poker?

'Amongst other things. Sometimes, when I was sitting on my mother's lap she would stroke my forehead and gaze at me with a tragic expression.' Adopting a high, pitying tone he continues, '"Poor Redsi, you think I'm your real mother, don't you? But I'm afraid that you were left on our doorstep by gypsies, and one of these days they might come back to fetch you."'

He lets out a cry. 'Arrggghh!' This time it sounds more heartfelt than usual.

'It made her feel good when I got upset, because that meant I loved her. Meanwhile I was nervously hunting for secret panels through which gypsies might come and get me. She tried this on quite often. Eventually I began to resist and would say, "It's not true." Whereupon she would reply, "It is true, as it happens, and if I'm not mistaken they're coming next week." She would prolong the torture as long as she could. There came a point when I had really had enough and retorted, "I hope they come as soon as possible, so I'll be rid of you."'

She was a convincing actress by the sound of it.

'If you gave her the slightest chance, she would start going through her role in *Murder in the Cathedral*, and she wouldn't stop before she had chanted all her lines. Luckily she didn't have too many, being in the choir.

T.S. Eliot came to all the rehearsals and if she had trouble with a line, he would change it on the spot. She followed him around in the hope of catching some wise words from the great man. But all she ever heard was a kind of oath that he uttered on seeing his car, "Those bloody birds have been at it again!" I assume that pigeons had been shitting on it.

I think she mainly beat me because she felt that having children had got in her way. That my brother and I were responsible for thwarting her theatrical career.'

We drive into Studland.

'This was one of my father's parishes – his last, in fact. He was already semi-retired. It was a very enjoyable time for him; he could bless the boats and sprinkle consecrated water on them. He was doing God's work and having fun at the same time.'

Redmond parks the car and leads me away from the church.

'He had this cross put up here. He wanted a kind of Anglo-Saxon cross in his village; he was prone to occasional fits of enthusiasm, and I think the idea must have arisen during one of them.'

The cross, which was erected in 1976, is impressive. It stands at least four metres high and is decorated with bas-reliefs, featuring Celtic motifs, birds, a violin, Concorde, mediaeval monks, the sun and moon, and a DNA double helix.

'He thought up all these designs. They each meant something to him, though I can't recall what. He loved birds, that I do know.'

What species of birds are represented on it?

'A dove, because of the Christian symbolism. I can't readily identify the others. The cross was made by local sculptors.' It is inscribed with the name of its main sculptor, Trev Haysom, a local quarry owner.

'This is spaceship earth and there are more Celtic motifs here. My father was crazy about the Celts because they were pre-Christian and therefore not bound by the rules that oppressed their descendants. There's a Christian fish. You know, the cross is more impressive than I remembered. It looks much older than it really is, and gets more authentic every year. It's already been included in a pamphlet on crosses in Dorset. Here are human figures. A woman. Hell. That certainly had to be included. He was a firm believer in hell. Eternal punishment featured prominently in his sermons.

I went to prep school in the next little town, Swanage, where I was a boarder. We used to walk from school to Studland, across the hills. That's quite a distance for small children; they really put us through our paces, I realise now. We walked side by side in a crocodile; you could torment yourself beforehand by wondering whether your best friend still liked you, whether he would want to walk next to you.'

Redmond points away from the cross towards an old house.

'At that farm we saw a bull mounting a cow. I must have been about ten at the time and was walking next to a boy named Strange, whose father was a teacher. We immediately realised what they were doing. Strange and I promised that we would write and tell each other when we had "done it". And we kept that promise, too, filling one another in on our first sexual experience.'

I'm losing my grip on the chronology; it seems more elusive than on other occasions.

Let me try and get this straight. This was your father's last parish. You were born near here, then moved to Calne only to return to school here, while your parents stayed in Calne? Then your parents returned to this neighbourhood much later?

'Right on every count. We had a teacher called Mr Fitzgerald, who always made sure that the boys stayed well away from the sea. We didn't know why until someone told us that he had once taken a group of boys to play on the beach. Four or five of them had found what they thought was a treasure chest and prised it open, but it was a mine. They were blown to bits. The story went that the only thing left of them was a single gym shoe. One of their fathers quit his job and spent his days pacing the beach in the hope of finding a trace of his son. He became deranged. Ever after that, Mr Fitzgerald kept the walks away from the beach.'

We enter the church of St Nicholas, where the record of incumbents lists the name of William Douglas O'Hanlon as the previous vicar. It is a tiny church, much smaller than the one in Calne.

'The vicarage is bigger than the church, perhaps three times as big, though once again, no one questioned this.'

In this church, too, a board displays the hymn numbers for the previous Sunday.

'I should feel at home here, but that is absolutely not the case.'

We step outside. Redmond points to the upper storey.

'There's the priest's hole. If a gang of robbers came, or an invasion or some other form of danger threatened, the priest would climb the ladder, crawl into the hole and pull up the ladder behind him. Provisions of food and drink were stored there, so he could lie low for quite a while. No one would have an inkling of his whereabouts, bar the whole parish ...'

Redmond has already briefed me on the Anglican Church hierarchy of vicars, canons and rectors. In Calne, his father was first an ordinary vicar and then a canon. In Studland he was a rector, which meant, as I understand it, that he was also entitled to some of the land in his parish.

'Let's go this way.'

He leads me across the churchyard.

'I want to show you a few graves. One of them has an inscription that reads, "Bellringer of this church". The other says, "Stonemason of this church".'

He does not find either of the tombs.

'This tree is probably as old as the church.'

We walk on.

I find myself face to face with his mother's grave, which bears the short inscription 'Philippa Katharine O'Hanlon 1916–2006'.

'We told my father that we had left lots of space for his name.'

I didn't know that she had died so recently. So she lived to be ninety.

'She had Alzheimer's. In her final years her mind started to go and she ended up living in the same home that my father is in now. He loathes being visited, but she liked people and was always pleased by company. Once I remember her opening the door to me and saying, "Hello? Who are you?" For some reason I answered, "I'm the Emperor of China." "How fascinating! Do come in."'

Redmond laughs in a subdued fashion, but in the deserted churchyard it sounds louder than it would elsewhere.

'Then she announced to everyone, "This is the Emperor of China. We are most honoured by his visit. Would you like a cup of tea? Chinese tea?"'

He manages to rein in his guffaw somewhat.

'She went off to make tea, but entirely forgot what she was doing in the process. She came back with a little bowl of something. "May I offer you some crisps?" In fact they turned out to be cornflakes.

The last stage of her illness was bearable, because she was pretty much out of it. It became amusing, up to a point. It had been preceded by periods of great anxiety, though, as she gradually realised that something was wrong. We went to visit her in hospital after she had been given an artificial hip. She pointed to my brother, whom she still recognised, and said, "Tim, one day all this will belong to you." I just played along with her, but he tried to put her straight. "No mother, this is a hospital." She got agitated, saying "This is not a hospital, it is my house." She called a nurse. "Please tell this man that this is my house, and that one day it will belong to him." The nurse backed her up, saying "Of course it is." Whereupon my mother said, "Now run along and bring us a bottle of sherry and three glasses." In a way it was wonderfully entertaining, but God was I relieved when I shut the door of her room behind me.'

So you can stand here now without emptying a Magnum into her grave?

'Oh, definitely. I keep a certain distance, though. I hide behind an old gravestone. About six months ago I came here with my brother. He stood at the grave and just talked about everything that had been happening to him, like his son, Toby, qualifying as a doctor. Meanwhile I kept a safe distance. I'm still frightened that a hand will rise out of the ground and grab my ankle.'

He started to talk to his brother about the past only recently.

'When we were small, he would stick up for me. I can still hear him calling, "Mum, please don't beat him." I always assumed that he loved our parents, though. But when we had to decide what to do with the contents of their house, it turned out that he didn't want a single thing. He had been traumatised too. My brother was never a great talker, more of a growler, but now that mother is dead and father is in a home, he chatters away non-stop. We have fun when we're together. He's sixty-six now, so it's a bit late in the day of course.

The idea was that he should follow in my father's footsteps, but instead he became a teacher. He taught at Sandhurst and the boys he tutored included Prince Charles. The prince complained that no one would give him a book about sex, and he asked my brother for one. The only book he could think of was *The Ginger Man* by J.P. Donleavy. There's a scene in it where the main character's toilet collapses through the floor below and its contents fall on the head of his wife. Charles thought it was the best thing he'd ever read.'

But.

Do you want to visit your father?

'No,' says Redmond resolutely. 'My brother rang not so long ago to say that we would rather not go there any longer. He clearly doesn't want to see us. There was a stage when he could still walk, but refused to go outside, and now his legs no longer carry him, I think. He just sits there all day. Never turns his television on. Never reads a book or a newspaper. When we went to visit him, he would send us away. I wonder what's going on in his head.'

Why is he so angry?

'Because he's surrounded by pagans. The newspapers are full of pagan stories. The staff bring him food, dress him, move him from his bed to his chair and then back again. He doesn't want anyone to disturb him and he prefers to remain in bed. He is ninety-seven, and he's been in the home since he was in his eighties.'

Would you say that his fundamentalism increased as he got older?

'Years ago my mother took him a set of my books. He told my brother that he would never forgive her – that it was the worst thing she had ever done in her life. Couldn't understand what had possessed her.'

So what did motivate her? You told me that she didn't like books.

'I've no idea. My father told my brother that if it had been up to him all my books would have been burned. Because they were pagan. He also believed that all black people were doomed ...'

So no visits?

'No.'

Quite sure?

'Yes.'

A walk of only a few hundred metres or so (past signs warning pedestrians of an aggressive and dangerous doe) takes us to one of the best-known local pubs, the Bankes Arms. Redmond wants us to lunch there on account of the special rooks.

'They perform tricks. They catch chips in the air and open bags of crisps unaided. They like to start off with a decent pub lunch and then sit around cawing.'

After placing our order we go in search of a table with rooks, but the birds are temporarily absent.

'Perhaps they only come in the evening. Perhaps the harvest has just been gathered in and they can find better things in the fields than chips.'

Perhaps they're trying to eat more healthily and have given up chips for the time being.

'People like it when a rook comes to sit at their table, though close up they tend to find them unprepossessing. I can't understand why: they're such fine, intelligent-looking birds. It's

Rudi Rotthier and Redmond O'Hanlon

considered bad luck to chase rooks off your land; the story goes
that if you do your house will fall down.' Redmond asks the
waiter where all the rooks and jackdaws have gone. The man,
an African whose French is better than his English, shrugs his
shoulders uncomprehendingly.

'There's a tip we can pass on to foreign readers: don't go
to the English coast thinking you're going to meet the locals –
you'll be shocked to discover that there's no one left who can
speak English.'

By the time we have finished the fresh crab salad (the menu
even tells you the name of the ship that supplies the fish and
shellfish), a few rooks do show up, but soon flap off with a

disappointed air, perhaps because they've spotted that we haven't ordered any chips.

When Redmond was young, pubs were the exclusive domain of men. He has seen them change into places where families are welcome, and where you find children at play, as we do now. Sometimes the world gets better, he concludes.

A child calls to its playmates, 'Which animal would you rather be?'

One of them answers, 'The biggest of something.'

Redmond leads me to a spot close to where the ferry should have docked, on heathland where he used to play as a child and watch birds. The vegetation is blackened by traces of fire.

'That's where my father moored his boat – a sixteen-foot yacht. We used to sleep on board. Waking up on the water was a real adventure. We would bivouac there for a week or so, rowing ashore every now and then in the dinghy.' He recalls the races in which his father competed. 'In the end he was banned from taking part, after twice crashing into the ferry.'

We get out of the car, picking our way through the sand of the dunes and brambles. He worries about my sandals. 'Are you sure that you want to have your toes slashed open?' A hide now stands on the spot where Redmond used to lurk silently between two bushes. It contains a logbook in which sightings are noted down and lists are made of birds. We peer towards Poole Harbour, mostly in silence, occasionally communicating in whispers. Earlier, Redmond had pointed out the island in the bay, Brownsea Island, the only place in the south of England where you can still find red squirrels.

'I'm sure we'll get to see some shelduck. They're not really ducks, in fact they're bigger than many species of goose. They like to nest in rabbit warrens. The sexes are similar, but the males have a kind of red knob on the top of their beaks.'

But the shelducks are not putting in an appearance just yet.

'It's high tide, which isn't so good.'

He thinks he spots a black-tailed godwit in the distance. 'I should have brought my telescope.' The few birds we can see are too far off for our binoculars.

Redmond leafs through the logbook. 'Winter is the best time of year for birdwatching here, and January and February are the best months. In January birds migrate here from the polar region to look for food. Good heavens, there have even been sightings of Goldeneye ducks. There's a freshwater lake nearby. You usually find an incredible variety of birds in places where there's both fresh water and salt water. But now's not a good time. I don't think it's worth walking over there.'

In the absence of birds, we whisper instead about the pleasure they bring when they are there.

'Nature is always satisfying, natural history never lets you down,' says Redmond.

In what way?

'Well, you might be feeling low and think you've seen it all, but then you come to a place like this, just sit and observe what's around you, and each time it's more beautiful than you remembered.'

Is that a feeling you want to pass on?

'Up to a point. I've never felt the need to capture it by taking pictures. Though I love photographing people.'

So nature is your private pleasure?

' Yes, I think that's a good way of describing it.'

He goes on browsing in the logbook. A grand total of 415 grebes have been recorded.

'You've got Slavonian grebes, which breed in Iceland and are quite dark. Then there are Red-necked grebes, which come from Siberia and are paler. I like to imagine that they look at the Slavonian ones and think, you sexy thing, where did you get that tanned chest?'

Do you think a life of observing animals and doing field studies would have appealed to you?

'I don't have the patience to sit still for hours carrying out observations. But I do get immense pleasure from reading about the findings of such studies and I think, who needs religion to talk of miracles? Surely the world of biology is infinitely more amazing? All sorts of incredible revelations are constantly coming to light. Do you know which land-based animals are the closest relatives of marine mammals? Darwin thought bears, because they like swimming so much. About five years ago, genetic scientists found out that it was hippopotamuses. When you think about it, it makes perfect sense. After all, a hippopotamus is a sort of embryonic whale, so it's not surprising they have common ancestors. Hippopotamuses have always fascinated me. Footage shot below the surface of African waters shows that they trot about on lake and river beds – I find the idea of them going for an underwater stroll deeply satisfying. They can also adapt their density so as to sink or rise, just like whales. When they come on land, both males and females mark their territory by excreting and spreading their dung over a huge area with their tails. A hippo's tail acts like a kind of shit-spreading fan; in fact, that's its main function. They never do it in the water, though, not wanting to dirty it.

Or take sperm whales – they can dive to a depth of two miles and then come up at the exact spot where they submerged. It's an essential skill, because they have to be able to find their young where they left them.

If this sort of thing isn't marvellous, I don't know what is.

That's the way to make science popular – tell some of these amazing stories. After all, there are enough of them.

The Dutch naturalist Niko Tinbergen was exceptionally good at that kind of thing. Everyone could understand his experiments. Take the one about herring gulls, for instance. Herring gulls have a red spot on their bills, and when their young are hungry they tap hard on that spot, to make the parent birds regurgitate fish for them to eat. Tinbergen wondered whether oystercatchers have red bills for the same reason. He switched the chicks of the two species. When the herring gull chicks started to rap hard on the mother oyster-catcher's bill she was completely taken aback; it hurt so much that she actually fell over. Oystercatchers have extremely sensitive bills which they use to probe mudflats. They simply aren't equipped to cope with a herring gull chick bashing away at them.

Tinbergen's genius lay in the fact that he carried out his experiments in the field, not in laboratories. Take his famous study of how sand wasps find their way back to their nests. He discovered that they used pebbles to orient themselves, and that if he moved the pebbles they would creep into the wrong burrows. He was exceptionally dedicated in his work. No one had carried out such thorough experiments since Darwin.'

Redmond once visited Tinbergen, after establishing contact through friends.

'I stayed in his caravan in Walney. The wooden blocks he'd used in another study to test whether gulls would accept egg substitutes were still scattered around. They came in different sizes and shapes, square and spherical, and were painted the colour of a gull's egg. The gulls weren't fooled by the square eggs, but did select the largest of the normally shaped wooden eggs to hatch – and they really were ridiculously large. Apparently megalomania is not confined to Homo sapiens. There are famous photographs of proud mothers perched precariously on top of their gargantuan eggs.'

Chapter 8

PREP SCHOOL

We drive towards Swanage, which used to be a kind of health resort for miners and people with tuberculosis, who came to benefit from the sea air. Redmond has fond memories of the Pines Hotel, where his parents used to dine and where, much later, he stayed with Belinda and the children. The hotel is pretty old, but by no means as old as the guests.

'That's why I like it here. Everyone is so much older than me.'

The sea view is breathtaking, but all the rooms facing the sea have been taken, and we are allocated ones on the less photogenic side. We have a view of the car park. In fact, we have more than a view. If I open my window, I can touch the nearest car and throw a ball of paper straight into a municipal litter bin.

Redmond is less fortunate. His window is firmly locked. Since there are no ponies to which it could pose a danger, we can only assume that the management is afraid of burglars, it being large enough to climb through. Redmond goes to reception and is allocated a different room. He returns triumphant.

'That's a breakthrough for me. It's the first time in my life I have ever managed to get my room changed.'

Why have you never done that before?

'I don't like to complain. I feel that I must resign myself to my fate.'

We offload the luggage and leave.

'Would you like a few caffeine pills?'

No thanks.

'Excellent! Nobody ever wants one. People reel away from me when I offer them around.'

I never take any pills on me, even when I go on a journey. I rely on finding something locally.

'When I go off anywhere, I always fix up a consignment of drugs in advance.'

In the event that I do have any drugs with me, I always give them away early on. Though since I don't know anything about medicine, I'm probably giving them to the wrong person.

'Marcellin [his guide during the Congo journey, RR] always got angry when I gave drugs to pygmies. He thought I should keep them in case we needed them ourselves later. In the old days Swanage was just a tiny hamlet, but masses of new buildings have sprung up everywhere now. The locals protest, but in a way it's rather wonderful. It looks like the Costa del Sol.'

In Dorset.

'Yes. The beach is disappearing, but they keep topping it up with new sand.'

So where are we heading now?

'For my prep school.'

Another place of horrors?

'Oh yes, worse than Marlborough College.'

The building is large, red and impressive, though on an infinitely smaller scale than Marlborough.

'I don't feel like introducing myself. It's no longer the same establishment; it's now a school for children with learning difficulties.' What was Forres School is now the Purbeck View School.

Why were you sent here?

'Probably because my parents thought the sea air would do me good.'

Once again, he assumes the role of tour guide. 'That's where we played cricket. I was invariably out for a duck. There's the chapel. My time here wasn't all bad; I played a lot of sport and got off to a decent educational start. My name was on the honours board, with the dates that I was here. When the school moved, the board went with it. Before the move, they even sent me an invitation to come and see it while it was still in place. Arrggghh! I didn't go. That was the headmaster's room. The dovecote was there – the school pigeons were my fellow prisoners. That was the art room. I see the dormitories have new windows. Each dormitory was named after an admiral, the idea being that it would inspire pupils to join the navy. If you were caught with chewing gum you were beaten, which happened to me a few times. Everyone wet the bed.'

Did you get beaten for that, too?

'No, they didn't mind that. We were six or seven years old, after all. They would put rubber sheets on the mattresses and no one considered it shaming, because everybody had a rubber sheet.

On the first or second night I invented a game. The gaps between the beds were just narrow enough to allow you to jump from bed to bed in the dark and hit other boys on the head with your pillow.

One night the light went on to reveal an immensely tall man, dressed in tweed, with a pipe in his mouth. I thought he might have come to give us some kind of treat – perhaps sweets. Instead he caught hold of me by my pyjamas and led me to a special chair. He had a rack, rather like a gun rack, which held a display of canes that he had personally made. For the very small children he favoured a broad model – a paddle, really. The thinnest canes were reserved for the sixth-form boys. He proceeded to beat me with the paddle. My buttocks turned black afterwards and I couldn't sit down for about three days. It was all right though, because you could show the bruises to everyone: they were a kind of badge of honour. The colour gradually changed from black to green.

Was there any sexual abuse?

'We were fondled and beaten, but I never heard of anything more extreme. With the exception of Mr Strange, my friend's father, all the staff – excellent teachers to a man – were homosexual. Mr Fitzgerald clearly loved his job, and French was exciting when he taught it. He could get even the dullest pupils to learn the language. I assumed that everything he did was typically French. If you had done well on the vocabulary tests, he would roll up his sleeves and say, "You may feel the hairs on my arm." That was the greatest possible honour that you could achieve.

At a certain hour you had to take your work to his room. You would walk round his bed and place it on a silver salver. He would be lying on his bed, a pink and white striped towel draped over his knees, with his enormous erect dick on full display. Not knowing any better, I assumed this was perfectly normal. I wasn't sure whether I wanted mine to end up as large as his, though. Unlike the better-looking boys, I was never invited to his room to watch television – he was the first person to have one – but everyone was treated to the sight of his penis.

These days, of course, you would be arrested. Much later,

at Marlborough, where most of the teachers were married and heterosexual, I once told everyone around me at an official school dinner that I knew what the French got up to. As I described the scene (even then failing to realise that it was abnormal) I could see the jaws of the assembled parents dropping. I've heard that Mr Fitzgerald is in the same home as my father, but I really don't feel like paying him a visit. Who knows what he gets up to these days?'

Who were the bad teachers?

'The maths teacher was the worst, as far as I was concerned. If you didn't pay attention in his lessons he would rap you painfully on the knuckles. Hurting children was clearly his thing.'

So this was where you, like the pigeons, were kept locked up all year round, except for fifteen weeks' holiday.

'That's right. You weren't allowed to use the phone, because it was hard to censor phone calls. Suppose you told your parents how miserable you were? We had to write home every Sunday. Not only were our letters read, they were pretty much written by one of the masters. He told us to inform our parents of the results of the rugby and cricket matches. You had to write about how you had achieved a glorious victory over a team that no one had ever heard of.'

Supposing you had told your parents during the holidays that you hated school and that you were beaten, wouldn't they have wanted to send you somewhere else?

'Absolutely not. They regarded beating as part of a boy's education and they always parried any complaint with "Worse things happen at sea," by which they meant, in the navy. Being beaten couldn't compare with being shot at or drowned.

My grandmother lived nearby. I would go and visit her at weekends, or when I had just had a particularly bad beating.

Although she had been a fundamentalist Christian, she had grown somewhat milder in her old age and would give me ten shilling notes. I can still hear her voice, with its Scottish accent, "Reddy, get me my med'cine." Her medicine took the form of a bottle of sherry, hidden under old clothes in her wardrobe. I would fetch the bottle and she would have a quick glass. "Mmmm. My sleeping pill."'

Was it an advantage at school that you were a vicar's son?

'It was public knowledge. Many assumed I was therefore probably very naughty, while others tried to embarrass me with idiotic jokes.'

But in those days people respected the vicar, just as they respected the doctor?

'That was indeed generally the case. But the vicar had to be worthy of their respect. If it turned out that he was an alcoholic, people would stay away from church. He had to be above suspicion, and that applied to his children as well, to an extent. I can still hear my mother saying, "What will the parishioners think?" To which my answer was, "They're not bothered about me. They've got other things to worry about."'

He thinks back to Mr Fitzgerald's erection and shudders.

'It was most impressive that he could keep it up like that. For some reason he was expected to marry the under-matron, a prospect that, given his inclinations, must have been unpalatable to him. They fell out and she left – much to his relief. So a new assistant nurse was taken on. A stunning-looking young woman; a girl, really, though she seemed very grown up to us. She was always around when the sixth formers were washing themselves; we had to get in a tub of cold water. She let us touch her breasts. One of the boys, Robinson, was very well developed for his age and already had pubic hair. At that time I was captain of the dorm and one evening he asked leave to absent himself, explaining "I'm going to sleep with the under-matron." That seemed quite all right to me, so I gave him permission without further ado.

Not long afterwards I was summoned to the headmaster to explain this. He and his assistant cross-questioned me in the library. But I was clearly so completely ignorant of the implications of what I'd done that for once I wasn't punished. I didn't even know what "to sleep with" meant. Both Robinson and the under-matron were sent away. She was such a beautiful girl that I'm sure she soon found another, better job.'

How were they caught?

'Incredibly enough, Robinson wrote to his parents that he had had sex with the under-matron, apparently in some detail. He was quite proud of the fact and thought that he should be rewarded. For all he knew, it was part of the curriculum. It certainly contributed to our education, because he was able to fill us in on every aspect of sex.'

What was a matron's job at your school?

'She and the sister would give us medicine, keep an eye on our diet and watch over our general health. They were the female presence at school, dressed in blue, starched uniforms and white blouses. Everybody wanted to be ill, because if you were lucky they would put their arms around you and you could nestle your head between their breasts. You got orange juice, for another thing, and the under-matron would come and tuck you in and give you a big kiss. That really did make you feel better.'

How did you get to be captain of the dorm?

'I think I was going through a successful phase in the rugby team. I could shove very hard if I had to; you don't need a special technique for that. As captain I was also supposed to dish out punishment, but I never did. Robinson turned up at

Marlborough College later. By that time he was obsessed by sex. For all I know he became a gigolo.'

He drives on to the next village, Langton Matravers, and shows me the rectory where he was born.

'That's where dear Rosiebud pushed me up and down the path in my pram. I loved her dearly.'

So you really were born at home?

'In those days women in labour only went to hospital if there were complications. The rest gave birth at home, attended by a midwife.'

The old coach house that stood behind the rectory has been turned into a museum. Its caretaker is keeping an eye on her disabled grandchild.

'Not many people can say this,' Redmond tells her, 'but I was born in the rectory.'

'Really?' the woman replies. 'How interesting!'

'Not really.'

She immediately starts to root among her not very extensive documents in search of information relating to Redmond's birth or his father's stint as the rector in the years immediately after the Second World War. Meanwhile, Redmond examines the exhibition. He finds a mention of Mrs Bartlett.

'She was the local witch. When my brother was knocked down by a bus, she came to tell us that he wouldn't survive.'

The volunteer manages to locate a pamphlet in which Redmond's father is mentioned as the incumbent between 1946 and 1951.

'I was only four when we left, but I have many memories of that time. For instance, I remember sitting in my pram behind the church and being told to pipe down so as not to disturb the rehearsals for the play that my mother was putting on.'

Outside again, Redmond lingers for a moment, gazing at the rectory. His expression is mild.

Do you have good memories of this spot?

'Absolutely. Especially of the kitchen and Rosiebud. My biggest enemy was the cockerel, who always pecked me. I recall him hiding behind a bush and attacking me, after which I ran crying to Rosiebud, who hugged me and comforted me. At that age, crying was still permitted. She asked, "Did you get a chickiefright?" Chickiefright was such a nice-sounding word that it assuaged my grief.'

We head for the coast. This part of Dorset has been dubbed the Jurassic Coast, and – along with the Taj Mahal – is a World Heritage site. The name stems from the quarries in which dinosaur remains were found. Redmond points to ancient fields that were terraced as far back as the Middle Ages. We pass a pub which, according to him, 'is riddled with secret passages for smugglers to escape through. In the old days they were full of barrels of brandy. Do you see that old church there? The customs office was next door.'

Why was this place so popular with smugglers?

'They used to land contraband from France here. Especially kegs of spirits, which were hauled ashore in lobster pots. Occasionally the smugglers would take pot shots at the customs men to frighten them off.'

We arrive at the car park at the top of a path leading to the cliffs at Chapman's Pool.

Some day-trippers are trying to persuade a dog to set off on a walk. Despite their cajoling, the dog lurks obstinately under the car, only to emerge when he is promised a ride in a carrier bag.

'It's not our dog, actually,' says one of the day-trippers apologetically.

Once again, Redmond is accompanied by a swarm of midges that circle above his head. This time he is less philosophical. 'Bloody females. They sting you and suck your blood so that they can lay their eggs. While the males just leave you in peace and help pollinate flowers.'

Each path used to be part of a network of smugglers' routes; perhaps some of them are still in use. A few hundred yards further on we find ourselves at the top of a steep incline.

'Belinda and I once ran all the way down.'

Do you fancy trying it again?

'No, I'd rather not. I need to get fit first.'

Did you ever work out?

'You bet. Before I went to the Congo I used to train two or three times a week.'

I cannot picture him in a gym.

'I was in pretty good shape; I wore army fatigues. First I would cycle on those idiotic bicycles that don't go anywhere, and after that I would lift weights. I had strong legs, so was quite good at weightlifting. After the Congo I never did anything like that again, which turned out to be a mistake, because while I was researching *Trawler* I injured my back. The crew used to lug heavy equipment around in the hold. I picked up something that was about half the weight they usually handled and managed to do my back in.

When my father became vicar here in 1946, there used to be a local man known as Two Barrel Bartner, a nickname he owed to the fact that he could climb this hill carrying two barrels of brandy at a time. One evening in 1967, when Belinda and I had just got married, we were going for a stroll round here when we were suddenly blinded by searchlights. The customs officers could see that we were a harmless courting couple, and we were left to continue our walk, but smuggling was still rife at the time. Some of the contraband kegs were hidden in the church. The vicar got a cut.'

What, even in your father's day?

'I'm afraid so.'

But you just said that the vicar had to have an unimpeachable character and abstain from drink.

'Storing smuggled booze was all right, though, because it was the parishioners who were doing the smuggling.'

Chapter 9

FOR THE LOVE OF DARWIN

Belinda has been ringing for several days now, usually just after our evening meal. I get the impression that she is surprised when I answer my telephone; she sounds relieved to have made contact. Redmond has his own mobile, but the only bleep it ever emits is the distress call of a dying battery. He has forgotten his charger, anyway. But I answer and pass the phone to him, so that Belinda can pour comfort, encouragement and tips into his ear. It sets her mind at ease.

Why don't you call Redmond directly? I put the question to her the first time that she rings. I haven't yet realised that his mobile has been forced upon him and that he steadfastly avoids using it.

'He has a love-hate relationship with telephones, which he associates with his mother. It was on the phone that she was at her most hypocritical. She would be talking sweetly to someone at the other end of the line, while simultaneously pulling faces at the children. Since then he has never trusted a single communication made to him by phone.'

Yet we talk almost every day through that mendacious instrument.

Later that evening I scour the hotel lobby for the Wi-Fi signal that seemingly cannot penetrate as far as my room. I want to get to the bottom of the secret mission of the Lord's Taverners and see whether the convoy of Harley-Davidsons whose path we crossed has been mentioned in news reports. I fail to find any such mention, but the Taverners turn out to be a charitable organisation based at Lord's cricket ground. Nothing in their mandate smacks of fundamentalism.

As I sit among card-playing pensioners, waiting for the light on my laptop to go out, a man slides out of his wheel-chair. To say that he is tipsy would be to understate the case. Bystanders applaud; the card players put down their cards and join in. With some difficulty the man raises his arms in panto-mimed triumph. A couple of his mates hoist him back into his chair. There is another round of applause.

The next morning we breakfast early. Redmond has told me that he needs an hour to get ready, but he is punctual and delighted with the wheelchair anecdote. He is even more delighted by his upgraded room, and by the waitresses who serve breakfast: all plump brunettes with plunging necklines.

'You often see that kind of pattern. The hotel owner or manager has a preference for a certain type, and he staffs his establishment accordingly. His taste becomes the house taste.'

Redmond has had a nightmare in which his cat Bertie was run over by a truck. Bertie was really run over once, and now it happens again in his dream. 'He was badly injured. I dashed him to the ground, intending to put him out of his misery. But then he turned up again unharmed, the ideal incarnation of an ideal cat. I was aware the whole time that it didn't quite make sense.

When Bertie had his real accident, I took him to the vet in a panic and told him to do something – anything – whatever the cost. He gave Bertie some kind of facial surgery which was very successful, but came with a whopping bill of £740. Belinda's father, notoriously frugal, was still alive at the time. I expected him to be shocked and to tell me that the money would have been better spent on his daughter. He just pondered for a moment, though, and then said, "He's been a good friend to you, hasn't he?" I thought I was hearing things.'

Did he have any pets himself?

'A cocker spaniel.'

How old is Bertie?

'I don't know exactly. About eight. A cat year is equivalent to seven human years, so he's still got some life in him. These days he sleeps almost as much as I do.'

And next year he'll be exactly the same age as you.

'We'll throw a joint party.'

Belinda, it appears from their telephone conversation, is not recovering as fast as she had hoped. 'Being insanely optimistic, she thought that she'd be back to normal in about two days. She rang the nurse, who said that she should take it easy for at least two weeks. I told her, "That's not too bad, I'd thought it would be at least six months before you got better." Whereupon Belinda accused me of being a drama queen.'

Is it her first operation?

'Yes. But. She's very good at putting me in my place. We were talking about our programme for today and I said, "I'm whizzing off to Oxford first. Then I'm whizzing off to Kent." She replied, "Your whizzing days are over."'

He and Belinda have devised a daily programme, which he and I have boiled down to a more manageable list. It includes the only item that I have proposed: a visit to Down House, Darwin's home. We must reach it before it shuts at five o'clock, because after that it is closed for half a week.

That was originally the only objective for today, but Redmond and Belinda think we should drive via Oxford. It will not be a huge detour, and it will enable Redmond to prepare for another of our goals: a visit to the offices of the *Times Literary Supplement*. He needs his key and identity pass to get into the car park, where a space is reserved for him. 'Actually I only want to take you there to show you my parking space.' He adds, 'Write down that we need to buy cat food. We mustn't forget to check the latest post as well.'

Didn't you leave a great pyramid of tins of cat food for your neighbour's daughter?

'I may have done, but let's not take any risks.'

He has a drive of many hours ahead of him. I am not at all sure that we will reach Down House before five o'clock, but Redmond is in a good humour and apparently ready for a marathon journey.

'This route is forever etched in my memory. Either I was bound miserably for school, or I was leaving its horrors behind, heading happily for Calne. In both cases, I associate these roads with profound emotion. Look, a jay. They're such beautiful and intelligent birds. They like to steal other birds' eggs. They also cache acorns and can retrieve sixty per cent of the ones that they bury, which is pretty good going. Much better than squirrels.'

Did you ever go to school or come home by bus?

'Never. I'd hardly ever used public transport until fairly recently. But now I've got a bus pass. I haven't used it yet, but I'm proud of it. I can travel free outside peak hours. Here's my plan: one day when the bus is empty, I'll get on and just keep travelling round in circles. I'll fall asleep; saliva will dribble from my mouth. I picture it as a kind of Magical Mystery Tour: by the time you start a new loop, you've forgotten the previous one. That way, everything stays fresh.'

Just past the ruined castle with the associated anus story we take a wrong turning. Or perhaps not.

'I still remember the way, but it isn't here any more,' says Redmond musingly.

Sounds like a reasonable excuse.

'It's a perfect excuse. But it also happens to be true.'

Did you ever intend your travel books to serve a special purpose? For instance, I might describe my aim as wanting to show that the world is different to what we expect, that it is more complex.

'Yes. I had something else in mind. Nineteenth-century travellers always gave the impression that they were alone on their journeys, whereas they were being led towards their goal by tremendous guides: people who were resourceful, clever and resilient. Darwin was no exception. You do find references to his companions in his diaries, but they make almost no appearance in his books. As the son of a wealthy doctor he was used to having servants, so he didn't tend to refer to them. Wallace, being a working man, had a rather different slant on life. His works do mention the individuals who assisted him. In fact I believe that, without realising it, by describing and appreciating local people he pioneered a new genre of natural history writing. You see the same thing in the works of one of his contemporaries, Richard Spruce, an English botanist who explored the Amazon. I wanted to be part of that tradition.'

But you're funnier than Wallace.

'At the beginning of a journey you feel strong and invincible. After a while, though, you start to realise how hopelessly incompetent you really are. Your companions, meanwhile, are

amused by the way you fall over all the time. They can't compre-
hend how anyone can be so stupid and clumsy. So they start to
treat you like a child that needs looking after; they protect you.
With a rush of relief you realise that you're going to survive after
all.'

We are distracted by the appearance of a convoy of tanks that
takes over the road.

'So there are still tanks in this country. This is better than
Dinky Toys.'

Why did you love Dinky Toys so much, actually?

'What I liked most was being master of the situation. You
position them and drive them wherever you want. You can play
at wars and decide who will win. Though I never allowed the
enemy to have more than a couple of tanks, of course. I could
never make the conflict entirely fair.'

We pass a pub called The Silent Woman. The sign shows a
woman carrying her head in her hands. 'In order to silence her,
they cut off her head.'

Is there a story behind it?

'I don't know, but my mother always felt affronted when we
came this way.'

We pass campsite after campsite. The locals call the tourists
'grockles', which conjures up an image of poisonous shellfish.

'Thomas Hardy's stories are set in this region, around
the market town of Dorchester. In *The Mayor of Casterbridge* he
describes a man who gets so drunk at a fair that he sells his wife
and baby daughter to a sailor. Disgusted at himself, he swears
not to touch liquor for twenty-one years. He does very well for
himself initially, but then his fortunes start to decline. The
story is really about a brawny farmhand, who represents the old

guard, getting into competition with a scrawny Scotsman who makes intelligent use of machines and modern technology. The former thinks he can solve everything by force and challenges his rival to a fight. To give him a fair chance, he ties one of his arms behind his back. In the end, the new man and the new machines win. Not the physical fight, but the fight for the future.'

The writers you studied, Hardy and Conrad, were both Darwinians.

'That was one of the elements in their writing that fascinated me. Maybe all great literature is underpinned by some scientific theory or other.'

We join a larger road, leaving the country lanes behind.

'Chaps used to speed along roads like this in their sports cars. That seems to be a thing of the past.' Redmond is more than usually conscious of the cars that are driving impatiently in our wake. 'My whizzing days are over.' We are overtaken by a sports car. 'With a young man at the wheel.' Redmond looks thoughtful. 'Well, not much above seventy. But he wants to impress his new girlfriend. The other driver behind me got so fed up that he's gone off in a completely different direction. But isn't the weather glorious!'

Once again we pass Coombe Bissett, the parish to which Redmond's parents returned after leaving Calne.

'I think the reason that my father got so depressed here was that he was unable to talk to a single parishioner.

There was a farm behind the vicarage. On one occasion the barn caught fire and thousands of rats fled in all directions. Rosiebud, who had gone along with my parents in her capacity of cook and cleaner, was frightened out of her wits; she stood on a chair and screamed. She hated it here, not least because of the rats.'

Did she go with your parents to Studland as well?

'Yes. She died shortly afterwards.'

Did it feel as if she was your mother?

'Absolutely. She always called me "boy", even after I had grown up. "Don't fret, boy." She would play with me. One of her legs was always swollen. I spoke at her funeral, mentioning that I still had all the Dinky Toys that she had given me. All her friends cried. She is buried in Northampton, where her family lived.'

Was she paid?

'Yes, though it can't have been much. She sent some of her wages to her son.'

Rosiebud is a strange name.

'Her real name was Rose Labram; it was I who called her Rosiebud. Her son was a church organist, but also an alcoholic. One day he was playing the organ decidedly the worse for drink, making a spectacle of himself. An attempt was made to calm him down, but he stormed out of the church crying, "Play the damn thing yourself then." That was the end of his career as an organist. When he was young he got a job at Harrods, in the music department. A woman came to complain about her gramophone. He said to her, "Why don't you just give it a bloody good kick, Madam?" He was sacked on the spot. After that he worked for Thomas Cook, as a purser on cruise ships. Unfortunately he was terrified of dentists, and when he was down to his last two teeth he got fired, because passengers felt uneasy talking to him.

This was a difficult route on a motorcycle. I had lots of accidents. The thing that ultimately put me off motorcycling was having to concentrate so hard that I ended up memorising virtually every bend. I began to fear that I was using up all my brain capacity on bends, leaving no space for other activities.'

It seems you were constantly getting into trouble with motorcycles.

'That's true. First in Marlborough, when I got expelled. Then at Oxford, where I was given an official reprimand.'

What was wrong with driving a motorcycle at Oxford?

'Motorcycles were generally regarded as plebeian. People looked down on you for driving one. But at Oxford the ban made sense, because if all the students had had them they would have paralysed the whole traffic system.'

During his student days, he and his housemate Douglas, the one who fled from the book burning, went to France together on a motorcycle and sidecar. 'If we got a flat tyre, Douglas would throw himself down on the ground and groan that he, too, was *absolument crevé*. When we ran out of money, we plundered the fountains that people throw coins into. He couldn't be bothered to clean the coins; they were still covered in moss when he paid the bar bill.'

Inspired by that journey, Redmond wrote a novel.

'It was my first travel book. I sent it to Cape, and Tom Maschler wrote back to me. I can't imagine that happening these days, the head of a publishing company taking the trouble to correspond with a twenty-year-old would-be author. He wrote that he liked the beginning, about the gamekeeper and life in Wiltshire, but that the later bits about Paris and hashish bore too close a resemblance to fifty-four thousand other manuscripts about hash that he had been sent.'

The manuscript circulated at Oxford. The student magazine published an article about it, headed "Merton Potporn". The authorities were none too pleased. I was hauled before the governing body of my college, which duly concluded that I had brought Merton into disrepute. I was sent down for a year. Just because of a review of a book that hadn't even been published. I wasn't allowed within twelve miles of the university.

After a while I wrote to ask if I might return, and was permitted to appear before the governing body again. It was presided over by the warden, a man called Robin Harrison, who had written a seminal, multi-volume work on the law in the ancient world, and looked the part. Its other members included an elderly rear admiral. I was rather pleased that they had devoted an entire meeting to me; it meant they regarded the matter with the proper seriousness. The warden asked me, "Tell me, Mr O'Hanlon, what exactly is your stance on hasheeech?"

In a flash of inspiration I hit on the desired answer, "Well, Warden, I think that it's all right for the Arabs." Whereupon he replied, "Very good, you may return." Rear Admiral Hetherington stood up and mumbled, "Quite right. I remember the time when my ship sank during the war and we ended up in the desert. We didn't have any water, and the local johnnies were smoking that stuff."'

Redmond's guffaw makes the Clio shake.

Was the novel any good?

'Its main achievement was that it got me a wife. Belinda loved it, made a special velvet cover for it, and things took off from there. Which convinced me, once again, that literature is a good thing. She loved the bits about farms and fields.'

He has already spoken a few times about Douglas Winchester, his great childhood friend.

I ask Redmond if he can describe him.

'Tall, hollow-cheeked. Impressive, extremely talented. His mother died young. At Marlborough he was a hippy. We used to hunt deer with bows and arrows. His father had a heating firm called Kingfisher. He wanted Douglas to see a psychiatrist, but Douglas of course wasn't having any of it. So his father invited a psychiatrist friend to dinner, hoping that he would be able to diagnose his son during the meal. The psychiatrist refrained from comment, but Douglas was on to him: the man kept looking at him in a suspiciously intense way. After everyone had gone to bed, Douglas removed the battery from the psychiatrist's Bentley, transferred it to his own car and drove to Oxford.'

Not an easy trick to pull off, I would think.

'No. And the psychiatrist wasn't very happy about it.

Douglas studied medicine at Oxford. He really wanted to paint, though. When he was twenty-one he inherited £21,000, which seemed like a huge sum at the time. He bought a boat, in which he hoped to go to sea, but it was a narrow boat, designed for canals, and it capsized when it was hit by the first serious ocean wave. So he gave up that idea. Then he hooked up with a girl who acted in the troupe that staged The Other Side of the Underneath. It was an early feminist theatre outfit and actresses were allowed to join on condition that they slept with the woman who ran the company once a week. Douglas found out. His girlfriend left him. He killed himself soon afterwards.'

Because of that?

'No, there were other issues. I have his diaries, paintings and photos. He would write interesting and bizarre things like, "My penis grows uglier by the day." He was deeply unhappy.

He had prepared his suicide carefully. He drove to London on his powerful motorcycle, an Egli-Vincent 1000cc, and parked in Holland Park. He walked to a place he liked in a copse behind one of the ponds, poured a jerry can of petrol over himself, lay down and set himself alight. He had written me a letter, posted just before his death, in which he told me what he was going to do. When it arrived we drove straight to Holland Park. By then it was all over, and the police had removed the body. But one of his school socks, still marked with his school number, 666, was hanging in a nearby tree. We found some of his hair sticking to the bark, and a charred lump of flesh where his foot would have been. I took the foot and the hair with me and put it in a Maxwell House coffee jar. It's now in my fetish room with an empty jar on either side of it, so that anybody around me who takes it into his or her head to end it all knows the score: if they kill themselves, I will collect their feet and keep them in a jar.'

It must have been a blow.

'Terrible. Later I wrote to the park-keeper and he wrote back to say that at first they thought someone had set fire to a shop dummy. Another park-keeper had just returned from Ceylon, as it was still called, where quite a few Buddhist monks were burning themselves to death as a form of protest. The only difference, according to the park-keeper, was that the monks had always tried to creep away at the last moment. Whereas Douglas had just remained still.'

Perhaps he was dazed?

'I don't know. It seems that the burning itself is not as painful as you would think. You suffocate, actually. Shortly after Douglas's death, the son of an acquaintance of mine committed suicide in the same way. He set fire to himself in a field. Afterwards he was able to walk into the house and talk to his father without apparently suffering any pain, while his mother waited outside for the ambulance. He died on the way to hospital. It's a terrible death; you don't stand a chance ...

Pfff.' He exhales in the silence that has fallen. Then looks in his rear view mirror to see that we are once again creating a traffic jam.

'It just gets worse. Now there's an old lady trying to overtake me.'

It is lunchtime, but also Sunday, which is a bad combination in rural England. All the pubs that we drive past are God-fearing establishments, whose doors will only open on the stroke of noon. In the end we find a place that is expecting a large party, but is prepared to squeeze us in beforehand.

I am increasingly tormented by the fear that we will not reach Darwin's house in time. Redmond is not particularly worried; on the contrary, he is in cheery holiday spirits. Without me realising it at first, he embarks on a detour that will add another hour to our journey. I don't know if he does it to tease me, or whether the urge to show me another landmark of the past simply gets the better of him. Whatever the case, he takes me to Milton Manor, where he lived for a while with Belinda.

It looks pretty impressive.

'At the time it was dilapidated and the rent was low because it didn't have central heating. Or furniture. But I did write my thesis here.'

Such furniture as he and Belinda managed to scrape together turned out not to be of very high quality.

'Anita, the one who set up Annabelinda with Belinda, stayed here for a time. She was a gypsy from Andalusia who had castanets and could dance the flamenco, and was married to the brother of a good friend. Shortly after Annabelinda was launched she fell in love with another friend of mine. They came to stay with us and managed to fall through the bed, which impressed me. Later, she moved to Padua to join him.'

To my relief we finally reach the toll bridge over the Thames. What is more, although the other cat had apparently managed to get itself locked in, and the neighbour's daughter is anxious to tell us every single detail of the story (and has absolutely no need of extra tins of cat food), we manage to keep our stop-off at Pelican House short.

I suppose you often get told that you're too efficient, I say to Redmond.

'Oh, all the time.'

Just as my fears about Darwin's house die down, Redmond starts to get edgy.

'If there's any hold-up along the way, we won't make it on time.' We get a worried phone call from Belinda, who is shocked to hear how far we still are from Down House. She passes on the news that Galen has bought a dinner jacket. 'We couldn't have gone any faster,' says Redmond. 'Though I suppose we could have bought sandwiches rather than stopped for a meal.'

Or we could not have driven to the house where he wrote his thesis, I think, but I leave this thought unspoken. I think he made the detour because he and Belinda have fond memories of the spot and he wants to be able to tell her that he went back. He imagines her beaming at the news. He himself beams in anticipation at the thought.

'God,' he says suddenly. 'I was so scared that I would lose her.'
During the operation?

'Yes, it was pretty major surgery and I couldn't bear the thought of anything happening to her. She's a wonderful person. She still looks so young and beautiful.'

When you gave that interview to the man from *The New Yorker* you said something along the lines of, 'I have done all kinds of idiotic things, I have behaved like a complete bastard, I was an absentee father, but I would justify all this on the grounds that I was busy writing and that literature was important. But now I've come to the conclusion that love is more important than writing.' How do you reconcile these things?

'I don't know if I can. I used to work twelve hours a day. But nowadays I'm not dedicated enough – or callous enough – to do that. I can't even work from nine to five. I have to be able to work at night.'

Do the children complain that they missed out?

'Yes. They tease me about it, but there's always a kernel of truth in teasing. In all the time that Puffin went to school, I never picked her up once. It got in the way of my writing. I did a bit better with Galen.'

You picked him up twice?

'More than that, even.'

Is it because of me that Belinda is convalescing elsewhere?

'No, the children were worried about what would happen if I was left in charge of her. They think I would get distracted.'

And would you?

'No, but ...'

You wouldn't feel comfortable in the role of carer?

'That's not the problem. They're judging me on past performances, I suppose. And they thought the farm, being very tidy, would be the best place for her. Cleanliness and order are better for an invalid than chaos and dirt.'

But.

'A colony of red kites has been released around here. In Borneo I invented a game that I now play on the way to London. I count the kites and if I end up with an even number, I will have a wonderful day. If I end up with an uneven number, the day will be disastrous. At first I counted just for fun, but, as is the way with thought experiments, I started to really believe it. One.'

You're superstitious.

'Yes. It's like with fetishes. If you've got one with you, you're invincible. That's a mindset that I can really understand.

Conversely, if you lose the fetish, you're suddenly powerless. Fear overcomes you.

And another one. Even.'

And another one. Odd.

'No, that's a crow who thinks it's cool to pass himself off as a kite. Three. Four.'

Did Belinda sound all right?

'Yes, she's resting and doing a bit of work for Annabelinda. She's sitting in the sun.'

Does she know that you are worried about her?

'I don't think so. That's probably just as well. Five. Oh dear ... phew, six.'

Seven?

'No, that's number six flying along with us.'

So it is still six.

'And it'll probably stay at six. We've left kite country.'

After a pause, Redmond remarks out of the blue, 'Darwin was incredibly tidy. During his time on the *Beagle* he learned to stow as much as possible in the smallest possible space. Did you ever read his comment that publishing his theory on evolution by natural selection was like confessing to a murder?'

The murder of God.

'Yes. He wrote in his autobiography that religion is innate, like our fear of snakes. When his son published Darwin's autobiography, he scrapped passages like that.'

Do you agree that religion is innate?

'I think that we instinctively need an explanation for everything, and God comes in handy. As the saying goes, man does not live by bread alone. But bread and science are enough for me.'

Nature is miraculous enough.

'Yes.'

I found his autobiography extremely readable.

'Yes, it's written very simply.'

By the end of his life he had become an establishment figure. He was given a state funeral. Hardly what you'd expect for someone who committed a murder.

'He was a nice man. His private life was blameless. People forgave him his theories. If he had left his wife or been an alcoholic, things would have been rather different.'

Would you rather have spent an evening with Wallace than with Darwin?

'No. By the end of his life, Wallace had become a Spiritualist. He thought that natural selection did not apply to man; he believed in eternal life. I think that any conversation with Darwin must have been incredibly exciting; his brain never stopped working away. Take earthworms, for instance. He started observing them as a child, and they continued to preoccupy him right up to the end of his life. There was a large stone in his garden and he tried to account for the fact that it was sinking into the ground. The only possible answer seemed to be earthworms. He calculated how much soil worms displaced and managed to account for the stone's subsidence.'

Is the stone still there?

'Yes. It's called the worm stone, appropriately enough. After that he studied barnacles for eight years. He wanted to reassure himself, be absolutely sure that his theory was correct. You could see evolution at work on barnacles. There's a lovely story about how his little son went to play with a friend, and asked him, "Where does your father do his barnacles?" He assumed that all fathers had a barnacle research station somewhere in the house.'

Do you think that Darwin was ever deeply religious?

'No.'

Darwin's father and grandfather were freethinkers. Why did he study to become a vicar?

'In those days you could only teach at university if you were a man of the cloth. It was an appealing life, too, in many ways. You got a nice house – you've seen the vicarage at Calne – and the church didn't place many demands on you. It was sufficient for you to have studied and to be a gentleman. You had lots of free time to study natural history and do experiments. Take Gilbert White, for instance, who was an early influence on Darwin. He was an eighteenth-century clergyman and pioneering naturalist who wrote *The Natural History and Antiquities of Selborne*, leaving him little time for his parishioners. White thought that swallows spent the winter hibernating in the mud on the bottom of ponds. Nowadays, we think that's strange, but what is stranger: that small birds can fly back and forwards to Africa or that they spend the winter at the bottom of ponds?

It is a charming book. He was a bachelor, and on his lone rambles he made important discoveries. He found out that house mice and field mice were different species. He was also the first to distinguish between chiffchaffs and willow warblers, which he did on the basis of their song. It's the kind of thing that we now take for granted.'

If God wasn't an issue, why did Darwin hesitate so long before publishing his theory?

'I think the real problem was his wife. Every evening she would kneel at the side of the bed and pray aloud for his soul. He knew his theory was a potential bombshell, and he was loathe to hurt her. Though he did stop going to church with her quite early on. He was rich, which helped. He didn't have to publish. While working in his study at Down House he found that he was distracted by passing carts. You or I would probably have moved the study to a higher floor. He had the road lowered.'

So he wasn't penny-pinching?

'No. He kept a careful note of his expenditure, but all Victorians did that. We have records of his budgets: so much for tobacco, so much for snuff. His snuff was made from coca leaves; no wonder he was so fond of it. He came to think that it was the snuff that caused his stomach upsets and flatulence, so he banished the snuff box to the corridor. However, that resulted in him having to get up every ten minutes, so after a time the box moved back into his study.

A complex man. I find him such an attractive figure.'

In a physical sense, too. He seemed to get better-looking as he got older.

'He became a wise old man. All Anglican priests were aware of natural theology. They were best placed to understand the impact of On The Origin of Species, the power of the idea of natural selection. After its publication, the suicide rate among this group went up. They were his readership, in effect. Message aside, his book made for more pleasant reading than the Bible.'

We negotiate the M25, find the right turn-off and are on target to reach Down House three-quarters of an hour before closing time. Redmond has visited it once before. 'Thirty years ago, together with Belinda and my parents-in-law. In those days it was completely deserted.'

Now there will be a queue a mile long.

'We shall see.'

As we drive towards the village of Downe, past encouraging signs like 'Darwin sports field', Redmond tells me that for much of the Second World War his parents lived within a mile or so of Down House, at Biggin Hill, site of the famous wartime aerodrome. He points out the airfield, now one of London's regional airports.

'Where are the Spitfires? They should be on display somewhere, surely? Thousands of planes used to fly over here during the Battle of Britain. Oh, there are the Spitfires. It's always a shock to see how tiny they are.'

His father was a chaplain at the time. 'During an air raid he leapt into a dugout and a group of WAFs jumped on top of him. He used to enjoy telling that story; he never seemed to realise how bad it made him look. The vicar diving for cover first, rather than first letting women take shelter.

Britain could never have continued to resist if Hitler had gone on bombing the airfields. One stray British plane dropped a bomb on Berlin, so Hitler ordered the Blitz on London instead. It was tough on the people of London, but it spared vital RAF aircraft.'

He turns off towards Downe.

'The tobacco industry gave pilots a free Dunhill pipe. It was the best advertisement imaginable. The fields we're driving past now are where Darwin did his plant experiments. It doesn't look like the farmland of a genius. But then no farmland ever does.'

These days there is a car park at Down House. We are just in time to be admitted. It is fairly busy, with lots of visitors from India and Pakistan, but there are no long queues.

Darwin would go on a short walk every day. Was that here?

'The sand walk? No, that's a bit further off.'

We pass through the first room. 'This is where his wife used to read novels to him.'

Do you understand Darwin's relationship with his wife? A woman who would pray for his soul and then make babies with him?

'He loved her very much, I think. Besides reading aloud, she nursed him and protected him.

In *The Descent of Man* he wrote that women were millions of years behind in evolutionary terms. Men had fought and developed, while women had stayed behind in the cave, as it were. He loved his wife, but it never occurred to him that he could talk to her as an equal. I've always thought it bizarre that men who couldn't survive without women nevertheless keep coming up with such theories. In his day, women did not have the opportunity of a decent education. They were not admitted to universities. They could learn to play a musical instrument, read and write, and they were praised for their intuition. That was the only area in which women could excel – in intuition, and in bearing large numbers of children. On the other hand, men and women are of course very different. Not to say superior or inferior, but just completely different.'

It was strange, though. He travelled round the world on the *Beagle* for five years and was fit and well the whole time, bar the occasional bout of seasickness. Yet when he came back he became a permanent invalid.

'His ill health was probably psychosomatic. This idea that he became a complete recluse after his return is a misconception. He did see those people who were important to him, while trying to keep those who bothered him at bay. His illness tended to flare up when commitments threatened. His gardener once said of Darwin's ill health, "The poor man just stands and stares at flowers for minutes at a time. He would be better off with something to do." Strange symbols appear in his diaries, once or twice a month. No one knows what they mean; do they indicate enjoyable sex or a satisfactory bowel movement? They do seem to allude to something he was particularly proud of.'

We enter Darwin's study.

'He personally archived thousands and thousands of letters here. It's funny; I remember the room as much bigger. Something doesn't feel right about it; thirty years ago it felt as if he still worked here. The smell was still authentic. Now the atmosphere has changed.'

The library contains the copy of *Das Kapital* sent to him by Karl Marx. Darwin never read the book.

'He hated big fat books. He cut them in two.'

Marx has survived intact.

I quote something Marx said about Darwin. 'It is remarkable how Darwin rediscovers, among the beasts and plants, the society of England with its division of labour, competition, opening up of new markets, "inventions" and Malthusian "struggle for existence".'

'I never heard that before.'

He wrote it in a letter to Friedrich Engels. Marx admired Darwin, but he was a bit suspicious of how conveniently his theories fitted English social constructs.

'There may be a grain of truth in it, but I don't think you can explain genius on the basis of cultural factors. Parallels certainly exist between the survival of the fittest and early industrial society, but the idea that biological science can serve social objectives leads to abuses like the Lysenko fraud in the Stalinist era. Darwin's theories are just as valid in other societies. But it is true, without Malthus there would have been no Darwin. Both Darwin and Wallace were inspired by Malthus' theories about the dependence of population growth on scarce resources. Darwin's theory builds on this premise: when there is competition for scarce resources, relative advantages become crucial.

The first edition of *On The Origin of Species* is by far the best. As the editions progressed, the message became more market-friendly, so to speak. The struggle for life was only introduced in the sixth edition.

There was a point where Darwin lost his nerve. It had been demonstrated to him that there was not enough time for his theory to explain the evolution of species. Fossil remnants show that there are sometimes periods of abrupt change, catastrophic events, but Darwin wrote that nature did not make leaps. He could not do otherwise, because leaps and catastrophic events pointed to a Creator. My father believed in the theory that the earth had been created on several different occasions. By way of experiment, if you like. When God became dissatisfied, He would allow life to die out and then He would start anew. That explained fossils, according to my father. Darwin was also concerned at the lack of fossil evidence to support his theory. But shortly after publication, around 1860, the gaps began to be filled in. Fossil remnants were found in Germany of an animal that was half bird and half dinosaur, the feathered archaeopteryx. We now know that the dinosaurs did not die out. Instead they became the birds that surround us now. A wonderful thought.'

Redmond becomes distracted by animal remains in the study. 'Is that a monkey's femur? And that looks like a bat. You know, this place feels less and less right. It's become a museum instead of a house.'

In the corridor we see a fossil of a giant sloth that Darwin brought back from South America. Or is it a copy? 'Impressive beast.'

Is it true that he didn't at first realise the immense significance of what he found on the Galapagos Islands? That he didn't make a note of which finch he had brought back from which island?

'Yes, and the same applies to the tortoises. He only realised at the last moment, just too late. He wrote to the governor to ask which locations each animal had been found in.'

We stroll around the pleasant garden. I look for the worm stone, but fail to find it.

Was he a keen gardener?

'Not as such, but he liked to experiment, for instance in growing orchids.'

I believe botany was said to be his weak side.

'Yet in that field, too, he made some interesting discoveries. There was one orchid which produced nectar deep inside the flower, at a depth of twenty-five to thirty centimetres. Darwin predicted that an insect would be found that was capable of pollinating this orchid. A few years later, a moth was discovered that did this very thing.'

Runner bean plants grow outside the greenhouses.

Shouldn't we pocket one?

'Just what I was thinking. Two.'

I hide two beans under my shirt.

We don't even know if the beans have anything to do with Darwin.

'He should have grown peas. You can learn much more from peas. Look, there's a wood pigeon. He studied those too.'

Shall we pinch some wood pigeons as well?

'Better not.'

I ask an attendant for directions to the worm stone. As I glance down, I see that one of the runner beans is sticking out of my shirt. The man remains impassive. Apparently we have overshot the stone. The worms are still doing their job, it seems, and it has sunk yet further into the soil.

Down House shuts its doors. We will spend a night at Belinda's farm, about an hour's drive away.

Once again we pass Biggin Hill.

'We should visit the chapel. I've never been there. There's a poem by my father on one of the walls: Ode to a Windsock.

God, what a time that must have been. The pilots prayed more than anybody and his chapel was always full. During the Battle of Britain my parents would sometimes invite pilots to tea. They were mere boys, really, and enjoyed these brief outings that reminded them of home. The appalling thing was that the average life expectancy during that battle was three weeks. My parents gradually learnt not to make friends any more, because they invariably lost them. Their self-imposed loneliness came to affect me, too, as I grew up. We always lived in such isolated circumstances; my parents would no longer admit anyone to their world.

During the Second World War, my father felt truly needed. Despite the horrors, it was his finest hour.

My parents had a dog called Roger, a cocker spaniel. Roger had a favourite tennis ball. The pilots would lounge in their chairs, waiting to be scrambled. They sat in a circle, with Roger in the middle. He would push the ball towards a pilot with his nose and the man would roll it back. Then Roger would push the ball to the next pilot, making his way round the circle. He drove everybody mad, but at the same time he took a little of the tension away. By the time I was growing up, Roger was an old dog. He still kept on rolling his ball, though, pushing it towards the drawing room walls. My father would say, "He's rolling the ball towards the ghosts of all the dead pilots."

Thanks to my parents' experiences I could picture the war vividly. I once met a woman who had got to know my father at that time. Perhaps she was one of the group that had jumped on top of him. She said that she had once danced with him on top of a roof. What strange times those must have been: incredibly young, semi-trained pilots being rushed to battle because their predecessors had been killed. All living in constant fear of death.'

Your father is suddenly much less of a mystery, I think. It's hardly surprising that he never got over it. What could he tell young men in that situation?

'He believed that they would go to heaven, because they were fighting a just war.'

A kind of jihadi mentality.

'Yes. That made it somewhat bearable for him. Perhaps those memories have come back to haunt him. He once told my brother that everything he had done in his life was wrong. Of course, that's the sort of thing people with depression say.

During the war he was also posted to Iceland for a while. I don't think my mother went with him. It was the base from which Hudson bombers hunted U-boats. All those pilots died. Their radars didn't work very well, and when the fog closed in they couldn't find their way back to the landing strip. When the kerosene ran out they would land on an iceberg and send out a distress signal. The signal would gradually become weaker and weaker, and finally die away. But when the call came for the very last plane to go out on patrol, the crew simply picked up their gear and left ... now that's true courage.'

But.

'I'm glad we pinched Darwin's beans.'

Are you going to eat them?

'No. I'm still not sure that they haven't moved his study. You know, we're not far from Chartwell, where Churchill used to live. He, too, suffered from depression. He dealt with it by building brick walls. It was the only thing that really kept him going. He built walls everywhere – very good ones. They made him an honorary member of the Kent branch of the Amalgamated Union of Building Trade Workers. When he felt a bit better he took up painting. A member of the union came to inspect his work and, although he was firmly opposed to Churchill's political views, had to admit that he was "a dammed good bricklayer". Churchill came up with some great sayings. "Dogs look up to us. Cats look down on us. Pigs treat us like equals." He was fond of pigs, and was also a member of the farmers' union.

That's where I bought Belinda's father his last ice cream. It was a Magnum. He had had a series of strokes and a collapsed lung, and couldn't open his mouth wide enough to eat it. I should have bought a smaller ice cream ... He died of pneumonia, or "the old man's friend" as it's called, which he contracted in hospital.'

Despite these thoughts of death, Redmond's mood becomes sunnier by the minute.

'I would drive down these roads on my motorcycle when I came to visit Belinda. With a beating heart. Just like now. We're nearly there. A beating heart.'

Chapter 10

THE FETISH ROOM

The old farmhouse is another world, with other inhabitants and other stories. It is indeed clean and tidy. Belinda, still the cheerleader of our journey, is reasonably mobile. She has asked a neighbour, Jason, to come and shoot rabbits and in the space of two hours he has bagged twenty-five on a tiny plot of land. 'We've been eating rabbit for a week.' It is off the menu now, though, and Galen is busy preparing a Jamie Oliver-type of fish dish. Happy to be reunited with Belinda and Galen, Redmond nevertheless immediately relapses into the role of the family ogre and grumbler: at least until Belinda points this out to him.

The farm lies beneath flight routes to and from Gatwick. We go and sit in the garden and watch planes. Belinda is looking forward to that evening's episode of a television dramatisation of *Tess of the D'Urbervilles*. I am completely unfamiliar with Thomas Hardy. Belinda, by contrast, has read virtually everything he ever wrote. 'When Redmond asked me to marry him, I said, "I've read too much Hardy to get married."'

Redmond and his son Galen

Were you frightened that he would sell you to a sailor?

'Not that, exactly. But absolutely everything goes wrong in Hardy's tales.'

'The letter that you push under the door disappears under a mat,' Redmond puts in.

So why did you get married?

'Because he kept on asking. In the end I gave in,' Belinda says.

'In the middle of winter I used to take her on the back of my motorbike to places that I fondly believed were romantic. Her feet pretty much froze off.'

'Whenever he's misbehaving, I tell him, you know that I never wanted to marry you in the first place.'

'I went down on bended knee to propose just about everywhere in Oxfordshire. You turned me down in ...'

Redmond attempts to remember the places in question.

'I turned you down everywhere,' Belinda recalls. 'I remember telling you to stay in your chair like a normal person.'

'In the end you said yes on Jarn Mound,' says Redmond. Jarn Mound is a romantic high spot overlooking Oxford.

'I couldn't withstand the siege any longer.'

'We didn't even drink in those days.'

'Not a drop.'

'It's hardly surprising that you turned me down so often.'

'Just when everyone was championing free love, we opted for security and got married,' says Belinda. 'Free love didn't appeal to Redmond – or to me for that matter.'

Redmond snorts. 'People would ask us, "Do you have an open marriage?" Whereupon I would retort, "No, we have a bloody tightly closed marriage.'

Belinda tells me about the farm. 'My family came here in September 1946 when I was six months' old. My parents struggled to make ends meet; the land was leased and they had no capital. But I grew up with a feeling of security; in that respect my upbringing was utterly different to Redmond's. I was most fortunate in that my parents were honest with me and extremely caring. They never tried to dissuade me from doing what I wanted; as long as I was happy, that was enough for them. I studied English, like Redmond, but when I didn't want to finish my degree, they didn't make much of a fuss. Can you imagine how livid Redmond's parents would have been if he'd tried that?

My parents told me to follow my ambition. They had promised to give me a pound for every year of my age if I didn't smoke until I was twenty-one. I used those twenty-one pounds to buy my first sewing machine, and that's how Annabelinda started.'

I suppose you then took up smoking?

'No, I never smoked. The twenty-one pounds was a helpful excuse when people tried to force cigarettes on me. It was a lot of money in those days, perhaps equivalent to two thousand pounds now. In my family, two children got this reward, the other two didn't. In the early days of Annabelinda I worked my fingers to the bone, just to prove that I could succeed at something. That was due to my own pride, rather than outside pressure: my parents would have been satisfied whatever I had done.'

Could you understand why Redmond's mother behaved as she did?

'I think she had probably been warped by her own mother, who passed on her insecurity to the next generation. In turn she passed it on to Redmond, and later tried to do the same thing with Puffin and Galen. At one stage I used to go to Swanage every other weekend, in order to give Redmond the opportunity to write. Puffin and Galen only recently revealed what a nightmare it was for them. She seemed amusing; very different to me: extravagant, an actress. I thought that she was good with children, but nothing could have been further from the truth. Children crave stability above all else. She would appear at the breakfast table and bombard them with choice: "Would you like some fruit, or shall I make you a fried breakfast? Or would you prefer pancakes?" Then her mood would change abruptly and she would refuse any further involvement.'

'There was never any peace and quiet,' says Redmond.

'Even when you were sitting reading, she would create a commotion,' Belinda adds. 'If you went to the lavatory, she would ask where you were going and how long it would take. When I grew up, we each had a place where we could retire in private. Redmond's mother wouldn't allow him any privacy; she would snoop round his room. His solution was to create a huge mess to prevent her from finding anything. Unfortunately it prevented him from finding anything either.'

Redmond pulls a face. 'She would comment aloud while

she was reading the newspaper, saying things like "How interesting". The idea was that someone would ask, oh, what?'

'She just liked people to look at her: she wanted to be the centre of attention.'

'It led to some wonderful moments,' Redmond recalls. 'Once she threw some of my stuff out of the window and I retaliated by chucking some of hers out as well. She didn't know what to do, carry on throwing or rescue her own belongings. Just at that moment a parishioner came past. Our possessions were scattered all over the garden; we had to go and pick them up in front of him, while trying to think up a plausible excuse.'

Redmond told me that his parents liked you, Belinda.

'I maintained the relationship with the family,' says Belinda. 'At a certain point, Redmond wanted nothing more to do with his parents. It got very complicated. Now Redmond winds Galen up, just like his mother used to wind him up. He's perpetuating his own upbringing. Galen needs a certain amount of distance from him. He's about as old as Redmond was when we got married.'

When he was sent down from Oxford because of his novel, Redmond came to live at the farm for a while. 'Three months,' Belinda remembers. 'Afterwards he was able to tell the governing board of the college that he was married.'

'And to a farmer's daughter, at that,' says Redmond. 'Which was definitely considered a good thing.'

He helped Belinda's father on the farm while he was there.

'I picked hops and raked hay, while at the same time trying to write. It was a romantic notion I had picked up from Tolstoy – his idea of the noble farmer paying off his debts with honest toil. I completely bought into the idea. But the reality soon turned out to be anything but romantic. I drove a tractor around, choking on diesel fumes and deafened by the racket, and when I was shovelling grain in the silo – barley was the worst – I could scarcely breathe. It did make me respect Belinda's father, though. I used to wonder why he spent his free hours slumped in front of the television, but before very long I found myself slumped there next to him. In the mornings I would think, why are we working so slowly? But by three in the afternoon I could no longer keep up with him.

The first job he gave me was to clean out the chicken run. It had never been cleaned out before and the shit had piled up so high that the hens were banging their heads on the ceiling. I didn't know it at the time, but cleaning out chicken runs is the worst of all farm chores. If you chuck chicken shit in your garden it kills the worms; that's how bad it smells. Rats flee from the stench. Anyway, I hung on in there and cleaned the chicken shed, meanwhile getting a lot of Brownie points from my father-in-law for not complaining. It didn't occur to me to complain; I thought that this was what farming was all about, but since then I've never gone in for hens.

When the chicken shed was clean, I was allowed to do everything except plough. Belinda's father thought I wouldn't be able to keep a straight line and that everyone around him would laugh at his crooked furrows and think he was hitting the bottle. It was an intolerable prospect.'

Belinda fetches a photo of Redmond's parents. His father is a bald version of Redmond. Or rather, it's the other way round: Redmond is a hairier version of his father.

'He's got his father's looks and his mother's character. He was the youngest, just like Galen. His mother used to call him Reddy.'

'That annoyed me.'

'Just as he annoys Galen with all kinds of nicknames.'

'I must call him Galen one of these days. That would be a first,' says Redmond.

During the meal, Galen, who is about to study agricultural science, gives a long, detailed analysis of the financial crisis. He speaks in the same precise way as his father and has a similarly impressive vocabulary. Redmond finds it difficult not to butt in, but he does manage to let Galen hold forth uninterrupted. When Galen leaves the room for a moment, his father says, 'I'm trying not to swell too obviously with pride.'

'He wants to be independent from you,' says Belinda.

'Well, he's doing far too good a job of it.'

This has been our least alcoholic day so far. When Belinda is present, Redmond drinks much less and far more slowly.

There were or are plans to move. There has been talk of Redmond and Belinda selling Pelican House and moving to the farm, converting one of the barns to make a library.

'It's a real dilemma for Redmond,' says Belinda. 'He feels perhaps he should move, but actually he needs Pelican for ... let's call it his stability. His identity.'

His, not yours.

'Well, that's not quite true,' Redmond objects.

'His, absolutely,' Belinda goes on. 'You only have to see what a tiny place I occupy in Pelican. He is there all day, of course, whereas I am only there in the evening.'

'Belinda's lucky with the farm. It remains as it was. That's a source of stability.'

'When you're feeling good, this is a wonderful place,' Belinda agrees. 'But if things get difficult, you are on your own.'

It is time for *Tess*.

'It always makes me cry,' Belinda warns.

We watch, comfortably surrounded by a nest of books, so that I could, if so moved, pluck Hardy's work from the nearest shelf. It turns out that the life of the main character is indeed nothing but misery. A senseless husband and a senseless world. Belinda largely manages to suppress her tears. We spend as much time watching each other's reactions as we do the television.

The next day Redmond shows me the barn that could be converted into a library. There are holes in the roof. It is a huge, lofty space. You could hold a modest ball in it. I cannot quite imagine where he would work. I can't think how you could heat such a place.

'Nabokov once said that when you move into a new study, with a new writing desk, it takes six months before you are entirely used to the room and can work without being distracted. Add on the time needed for renovation, which could take anything up to one or two years. By the time it's all fixed up, I'll be dead. But there is certainly enough room for all my books, which was what prompted the plan in the first place. I could install my library here and the rest of the farm could remain as it is. The sale of Pelican House would finance the renovation, though there wouldn't be much left over.'

According to Belinda, the decision has already been taken. They will continue to live at Pelican House. But Redmond still seems to have his doubts.

'I'm glad that you agree I'd be better off staying at Pelican.'

I have said nothing of the kind, but he is so certain of his claim that I wonder whether I have shown some bias without being aware of it. I immediately qualify the pronouncement that I believe I have not made. On the other hand, I say, it might do you good to pry yourself loose from your environment.

Nothing can shake Redmond's impression that I am fervently in favour of Pelican House.

Can Belinda cope with the chaos there?

'Up to a point she, too, found that liberating. Her parents always insisted on everything being in its place. I'm beginning to understand that now, mind you. When the children move things at the farm, it can be very time-consuming trying to locate them. So it seems a good idea to hang your keys where you found them in the first place. Belinda says that when she retires, she will sort Pelican House.'

This is clearly a contentious issue.

'I have told her that she is not allowed to throw anything away. I got the impression she agreed. But I think I'm going to have to stand over her with a gun, just in case. She says it needs a thorough sorting out because it's unfair to land the children with the mess.

When she came round after the operation she was pleased to see me, and we sat hand in hand. The next day I came in with a bag full of things. The first thing she said was, "Oh, please don't make a mess." She didn't want her pristine surroundings to be cluttered up.'

How did you meet Belinda?

'She came to my room at Merton College along with Terry, who was her boyfriend at the time. Terry was a small youth who smoked a lot of hash and played the guitar well – he went in for Bob Dylan, Woody Guthrie and the old blues. According to her I impressed her favourably because I had a pair of Wellington boots in my room and a book that had nothing to do with literature: A Paddling of Ducks by Dillon Ripley. It was the farmer's daughter in her.'

A few minutes later I ask Belinda a similar question: what attracted you to Redmond?

'He was different, and he made me laugh. He had an original take on life; different and intense. And I liked the fact that he had Wellington boots in his room.'

It is time to leave again. We are starting on our last long trip. Galen has printed out a detailed route description. We will first drive to London to visit the *Times Literary Supplement* offices – or at least Redmond's reserved parking space – and then travel on to Pelican House. Belinda is especially keen for us to visit the TLS. 'It has played a crucial role in Redmond's life.' The previous evening, after *Tess* was over, she cautioned him, 'Now you're going to have a good long sleep and then it's off to the TLS.'

'When Redmond had finished his doctoral thesis, he had no idea what to do with his life,' Belinda told me. 'In New York I met Jeremy Treglown, the editor of the TLS. I explained how depressed Redmond was, and Jeremy got him on board. At first he used to go every week, then every fortnight and now he goes once a month. Suddenly he had a social life again, and used the telephone to charm or persuade people.'

That instrument of mendacity?

'When he wants to, he's quite capable of using a phone. He's so happy there. He's been there now for twenty-five years, perhaps even longer. One of the old guard. He always takes Crunchie bars for everyone.'

'And Flakes,' Redmond corrects. 'Chocolate flakes, nowadays. They're easier to bite into.'

Leaving the farm, we drive through the little town of Tunbridge Wells. With some difficulty – our confusion being compounded by Galen's extraordinarily detailed route map – we find the road to London.

'Belinda looks well.' He says it with an air of relief. 'They seem happy; they're probably relieved to be left alone again for a bit. TLS here we come.'

When you got your job at the TLS, what was it that appealed to you so much?

'I could ring all my childhood heroes and, by lying slightly, immediately get their attention. I would ring the secretary of a Nobel prizewinner and say that I was ringing on behalf of *The Times*. There would be a sharp intake of breath and she'd say excitedly that she'd get back to me directly. Half an hour later I would be talking to E.O. Wilson. Or Stephen Jay Gould. What's more, they would listen to me and be prepared to do what I asked. To write the review that I wanted.'

But in the end people must realise that the TLS is not the same as *The Times*.

'It *is* the same. The TLS is better than *The Times*. You just mustn't start off by broadcasting the fact that it never sells more than 60,000 copies, eleven of which are in China.'

Redmond is distracted by a Greater Spotted Woodpecker.

'Richard Dawkins had written a piece about Peter Medawar, the only scientific hero that Marlborough College has ever produced. He got the Nobel Prize for his work on the immune system, I believe. The French literature editor, who is either an anarchist or a closet Christian, but in any case a somewhat caustic type, had headed the article, "Loose Cannon on Deck". It was completely misplaced.'

Dawkins, author of *The Selfish Gene* and *The God Delusion*, has long been a friend of Redmond's. 'He was so furious that he stormed over to Pelican House. It was very hard to persuade him to sit down. We plied him with tea or wine, but we couldn't placate him. The heading had been added without my knowledge, and I was as unhappy about it as he was. I fetched my gun and handed it to him. He held it awkwardly and looked about him wildly, apparently at a loss to know what to do. I said, "If you are that unhappy about it, shoot me." For a second I thought that he might. He's never forgotten the incident.

He probably thought, that's literary types for you. He doesn't like the way we all kiss each other. At Ian McEwan's sixtieth birthday party he sat a little way off, looking uncomfortable. I said, "Richard, I have something private to say to you." He leant forward, whereupon I gave him a big wet kiss on his cheek. He is so serious. But he does write wonderful books.'

Redmond chews over the conversations of the previous day. 'I must remember to stop calling Galen "my little budgum".'

What does it mean, anyway?

'It's an affectionate term for a newborn rabbit. He finds "pumpkin" less off-putting.

Helga, my psychiatrist, often tells me, "You've put a lot of energy into your work. Now put some energy into your family." The thing is, I think I'm becoming increasingly convinced that there's nothing left to say. It should be possible to write about Orkney, but what is the point? Is it worth putting in all that effort?'

You could write something autobiographical. You're not exactly short of material, to judge by what you tell me.

'That would be too painful.'

I thought you said that pain was a necessary precondition for writing?

'There's a limit to the pain one can take.' He exhales loudly. 'Sometimes I wake up in the morning and think, what a pity that I didn't die in the night.'

That's not very nice.

'It certainly isn't.'

Why do you think that?

'Because at moments like that I feel, I've done it all, now. That's terrible.'

It is also a self-fulfilling prophecy. You've done it all as long as you don't start on something new.

'That's what Helga always says. I tell her, "If we move to Kent, I may never write again." Whereupon she retorts, "If you want to write, you will write." Ha!'

Why not write about nature, I suggest after a pause. Not many have the gift of bringing the natural world to life on paper.

'It's kind of you to say so.'

That's what you do at the TLS, really.

'Yes. It's a legacy of the books that I read as a boy, including the Collins New Naturalist series. Reading about natural history mustn't be a chore, it should be unalloyed pleasure. When I started studying English, it became even better: a stolen pleasure. Reading about natural history was completely pointless as far as my studies were concerned, so I could feel deliciously guilty about it.'

But.

Have you any idea how many copies of your books have been sold?

'Not the foggiest. I never ask, in case it's only ten. I believe that my books have been translated into twelve languages. Starting with Dutch, then French, German, Spanish, Polish and Bulgarian ... I was told I would have to go to Bulgaria if I wanted to collect royalties in that country, but I never got around to it. Into the Heart of Borneo was published in China, and Congo Journey is doing well in Japan, because it has a bit in it about Japanese scientists studying chimpanzees.'

I gather you are selling very well in the Dutch-language area.

'Yes. I've been on Dutch television a few times, which helps. People recognise me in the street. In Amsterdam, a woman with a pram came up to me and asked, "Are you the writer who ..." I immediately said that I was. For all I know she was confusing me with a writer of children's books, but I didn't give her enough time to explain. My favourite encounter was when a musician from the Concertgebouw Orchestra asked me for an autograph. He pulled out his wallet in search of some paper and as he opened it, out fell photos of naked men with gigantic penises. "This is embarrassing," he said. I answered, "Not at all, look at the size of that one!"'

You have to take your fans as they come. I helped him pick up the photos, while passers-by gave us some odd looks. I enjoyed it immensely; I wasn't at all bothered by the photos. They weren't mine, of course.'

By now we have reached the periphery of London and the traffic is slowing. Redmond asks me to remind him to pay the eight pound congestion charge.

How do you pay that?

'By telephone. I need to take a pee. Shall we have half a pint somewhere? Stick your arm through the window and flash your most winning smile.'

The line of cars parts like the Red Sea. I put it down to my arm.

I'll take Galen's route description with us to the pub.

'Good idea. If the car is stolen, we will have lost the car but not our way.'

In London we get comprehensively lost. Redmond had hoped to reach the TLS by midday; he wants to lunch with his colleagues in Zucchero.

'That's where I always go.'

You are a creature of habit.

'Yes, I find fixed routines very comforting. I like people to know me. I don't want them to be startled when I come into a room. That's why I love my TLS car park pass so much. I drive through London in all its terrifying anonymity and suddenly even the machines recognise me.'

We reach the car park entrance at least an hour later than he had planned; it is nearly two o'clock. He waves his pass and the door flies open. We descend.

'This level is reserved for the big cheeses.'

We descend yet further.

'The people who park here are still pretty high up the tree.'

We reach the rubbish bins and descend yet another level.

'This is me. Bay H7. It's been reserved for me for about three years now. Can you imagine how pleasant it is, after a month in Pelican, to find a spot that has been specially reserved? I usually come on Thursdays. That's a calm day. I can't foul up too much. I leave for London around four or five in the morning and return after the evening rush hour.'

Today, however, is Monday and busy. There is an air of civilised stress. Everyone is friendly; kind, even. But they are also instantly distracted by pressing concerns. Lunch is being skipped or has already been eaten. We leave for Zucchero's as a party of two.

The restaurant is almost empty, but Redmond's favourite table is not available. However, the proprietor's enthusiasm makes up for the disappointment about table six. Redmond orders zucchini del mare. I go for the pasta vulcano. As we eat, he tells me more about the TLS.

'Everyone there has a bit of a history, but no one ever leaves

– except for novelists like Alan Hollinghurst and Martin Amis. Hollinghurst was a very precise editor. He would sit there all day tinkering with semi-colons, then he would go home and bash out three hundred words or so about sodomy on a tiger skin. Martin, meanwhile, claimed he spent the day removing improper words from other people's manuscripts, while devoting his evenings to cramming as many improper words as possible into his own. For a while, he was full-time fiction editor.

The TLS is still the leading journal in the field of literature. We review as many books as possible, the idea being to cover everything of significance. The other periodicals, the London Review of Books and the New York Review of Books cop out by placing a few good, long articles. Libraries take their lead from the TLS; they buy every book that it reviews. Or they used to, until they were hit by cuts.

Sometimes books don't get a mention, despite being worth it. I occasionally send a book to a professor who hangs on to it for six months and then doesn't review it. That's pretty bad. If it makes it into paperback, it does then get a mention, which must be poor comfort for the author.

I find that it's the old academics, the ones with one foot in the grave, who produce the best work. You have to watch out that they don't end up with two feet in the grave in the process, mind you. I once asked Bernard Lovell, the famous astronomer, to review a book and he was able to criticise the author because he had actually been present at some of the historic events it described.'

The padrone is not disposed to close, though even table six has now been vacated. We order coffee.

Have you ever thought of stepping out of your books, or at least being less obviously present, like Norman Lewis?

'It is largely a technical matter. I believe in letting readers know fairly early on whose skin they have to creep into, as it were. They need to know the character and to understand your thought processes. So there is indeed something of me in the narrator, but I try to pare it down as much as possible, leaving room for readers to take my place. The idea is for them to feel as lost as I did in the Congo, as fascinated by that alien world. The narrator must be drawn with broad strokes to permit general identification. If you don't watch out, you present yourself as too strong and too omniscient; you end up looking arrogant. It's better to give your best thoughts and jokes to other characters. That's one of the reasons why I like to have a companion with me, ideally someone who knows a lot about science.'

I think a companion would prevent me from truly getting to know the region I'm travelling in.

'But I don't go on those kind of journeys. I arrive with tons of attractive equipment at a grotty airport. If I travel alone, I can't possibly transport it all from A to B without half of it being stolen. And while I'm trying to establish what's been pinched, the rest will probably disappear as well.'

So it's more a practical consideration? I thought it was because you needed a sounding board.

'It's a bit of both. Lary [Shaffer, in *Congo Journey*, RR] and Luke [Bullough, in *Trawler*, RR] were ideal companions. Luke claimed that he had never said as much in his entire life as he was alleged to have done in the book. But he knew all that stuff.'

You attributed sentences to him that you had thought up.

'Yes, but everything that he said in the book was something he knew. Or would have known if he had read the books I've read. He was tremendously knowledgeable about the ocean. The rest of the trawler's crew respected him once they had seen him in action.'

Was he upset?

'Absolutely not. After our journey he took my advice and went in search of a wife. He fell for a district nurse on the Shetland Islands. She had a mobile phone, so he bought a mobile phone too. They became an item. But she couldn't bear the fact that Luke talked about former girlfriends in the book, and she asked me to scrap those passages, which I refused to do. Whereupon her father tried to prevent excerpts from the book from being broadcast on the BBC, claiming that it would upset Luke to the point where he might commit suicide. There was a lot of fuss around that time about a scientist involved in the Iraq affair who had committed suicide and the BBC took the complaint seriously, even though they ultimately dismissed it as absurd. The woman wrote me a letter in which she wondered how patients would react if they knew that the district nurse's husband had had sex before marriage. I wrote back saying that one wouldn't want to marry a virgin, and that she should worry less about what people thought ... there's no surer way to ruin your life. Luke's parents did appreciate the book; they came to a talk in Aberdeen.'

It must be embarrassing when your travelling companions read your book. Their memories differ from yours.

'Yes. And their self-image differs from my image of them. Lary said I had made him more intelligent than he was; that he knew more in the book than he did in reality. "I've been turned into some bloody fictional hero!" But luckily this exchange took place at his house when some old friends were visiting. One woman said, "When I read your book, I thought, that's my Lary." Perhaps I should have changed the names. Jason [Schofield, the captain in *Trawler*, RR] thought so. But if you do that, the book suffers. You lose your self-respect if you get too far away from what really happened.'

V.S. Naipaul appears to have made quite a few changes in his travel books.

'I loathe his travel books. There are very few writers that I truly can't stand, but he is one of them. What do you think?'

Some of his books are magnificent. *Among the Believers*, for instance. He knew what was going on in Iran about a decade before anyone else did.

'I haven't read that. What I object to is his moaning. I read one of his books about Africa. He travels somewhere in search of crocodiles, returns before he makes it to his destination and moans about the hotel and the food. That is so trivial. I think his novels are good, though. *A Bend in the River* and *In a Free State*, for instance. But they always have a repulsive element. Spitting in vaginas and so on. I certainly wouldn't like to be one of his characters.'

Are Thubron and Lewis your favourites?

'No, my ideal travel book is actually *Dead Souls*. I've never been able to find the liveliness of Gogol's writing in any ordinary travel book. Of course, at the same time it's also a wonderful novel.'

Gogol as travel writer; it's an interesting notion.

'Yes, the ultimate aim is to write something deep and Russian, surely? That's what I tried to do with *Congo Journey*.'

Is that your masterpiece?

'Absolutely.'

When you're travelling, do you write down sentences that you already know will be included in the book?

'No. I make notes in the evenings and in the mornings I hold up the expedition for an hour in order to write them up. You can't spend more time on it than that. I give my companions the impression that I'm writing a letter to Belinda, along the lines of "hello darling, we're now travelling towards the southeast". Things that she doesn't want to know.'

And that you wouldn't be able to send her.

'No. But somehow or other a letter creates less suspicion. Everyone writes the odd letter. Not everyone wants to write a book.'

How much remains of those notes after seven years of writing?

'Everything. I expand the notes. I respect the chronology and the places. But the dialogue ... that's why a book like that is partly fiction. When you travel through the jungle there is no dialogue. You grunt and curse. You grind your teeth. You compromise the dialogue, adding bits together here and there. As you write, the characters start to talk in your head. But all the events that are described really happened. As far as I'm concerned, that is the pact with the reader. Otherwise you end up with a novel.

In *Into the Heart of Borneo*, after Fenton had nearly drowned, I wanted to release the tension by introducing a blue butterfly. The butterfly had appeared earlier, though, fifteen miles down-stream from the place where Fenton met with his accident. At times like that I find myself thinking that there are perhaps three people who would know the difference – but I still can't bring myself to do it.'

Would you have introduced the blue butterfly if it could have appeared at that spot, but didn't?

'On reflection, no, I couldn't do that either. The events have to be real.

When *Trawler* was launched we gave a party at Pelican House. Jason, the captain, was there. He is much taller than me, a massive man in peak condition. His thighs and calves are so huge that he has to buy jeans five sizes too large and cut them off at the bottom. He was mobbed by women poets and novelists, and female publicity staff from Penguin. At some stage he shook Martin Amis by the hand. It was fascinating to see Martin's little hand in his enormous paw. He had no idea who Martin was. Martin asked him, "Is life on a trawler really perilous, or did Redsi exaggerate the danger?" Whereupon Jason answered, "It's not dangerous at all. Last week our sister ship sank. Not a single crew member drowned. The helicopter got there just in time."

Terry Wogan was there, and Jeremy Paxman.'

How do you know them?

'I was on Wogan's show, and if a guest doesn't turn up at *Newsnight*, it sometimes occurs to them to invite me as a replacement. They wanted to do an item on Ranulph Fiennes and explorers. I had warned Jeremy that I had already had a few. He said, "Don't worry about that, the car is on its way."

It was claimed that Fiennes was walking to the North Pole, or it may have been the South Pole, in the service of science. I said: "His exploits are all about extreme sport, not science." Though I greatly admire explorers who made important finds, like Du Chaillu, who was the first Westerner to discover the gorilla, in 1855. He exhibited the gorilla with leaves covering the spot where his genitals should have been. Du Chaillu had cut off the gorilla's penis – because it is only two-and-a-half centrimetres long when fully erect. "Which may be because gorillas have small, stable harems, whereas chimpanzees are well endowed because they live in large promiscuous groups." Paxman hurriedly rounded off, "Well, I wouldn't know about that. But I can tell you that the FTSE has gone up, and this is what tomorrow's papers are saying ..."'

We drive away from London, initially at a snail's pace.

'I usually leave around half past seven. But the traffic isn't too bad at the moment. I know this route, too, so I don't think that we'll get lost this time. When I return from the TLS I feel as if I have achieved something important.'

Father has been to work and comes home content with his day.

'Yes. It is extraordinarily satisfying, and the pleasure is all the purer because no one knows that you were the editor who oversaw a particular article. That makes me intensely happy. The TLS is a place where you feel that ideas really matter, that intellect is important. I come home and crawl into bed with Bertie and sleep the clock round, then wake to find my elation has evaporated. The TLS also allows me to read about science or leaf through periodicals like *Nature* or *New Scientist* without feeling guilty.'

Why should you feel guilty about that?

'Let me put it like this: I can hang a lot of my activities on the TLS.'

Would it suit you better if you went back to going twice a month?

'Perhaps it would.'

Have you ever been extremely poor?

'Oh yes, when I was a student. We lived on eggs, apples and beans. We didn't drink. If Belinda hadn't been there, I would have lived off tinned sardines. They contain everything you need – if you can digest the bloody things, that is. Professor John Bayley, a man I admired and who was extremely chaotic, lived on sardines. But he did insist on them being in olive oil.'

That's more expensive, of course.

'A few pence. If I wanted to give my intelligence a brief boost I would eat sardines in olive oil. Belinda favoured eggs. Sometimes we ate dogfish. Belinda supported me financially in those days. After I had finished my studies, I had two years to write my thesis. I chose nineteenth-century literature and spent almost the entire time reading. I found that literature was full of scientific knowledge. But the average don teaching literature at Oxford fifty years ago would have preferred to study theology, not science, and avoided science like the plague, loathed it even. They were the sort of people who would say, "In chemistry we were taught that humans were made up of ninety per cent water," while rolling their eyes in exasperation. Apparently that boded ill for culture, because how could a body that was almost entirely composed of water be capable of philosophy?

I therefore expected my thesis to be badly received. After it had been discussed I was asked to remain in the room; the dons all sat round the high table looking grave and averting their gaze from me. That didn't seem like a good sign. I thought, I'm not going to get six of the best again, am I? Not at university. Bastards. Not again. But they stood up and shook my hand. When I went out I thought, I'll be damned. It was almost as good as having a beetle named after you. Their approval of my papers and thesis meant I could get my M. Phil., in this case with congratulations.'

He was given a job teaching English literature at Hertford College.

'It turned out that I had taught the wrong century. Well, you know the state of my house. The letter with the programme description had fallen down the back of the sofa or something and for a year I taught Hardy and Conrad, whereas I was supposed to be teaching twentieth-century literature. It all came out just before the examinations. I was fired and realised straight away that I could never work at a university again. It's not the kind of thing people forget. In a way I was relieved.

Some time later I ran into a former student, who didn't seem to bear any rancour; she, at least, had forgiven me, having found a career in publishing.'

Did she fail her degree?

Redmond outside Hertford College, where he taught the wrong century of English literature

'No, the students still got their degrees as it was clearly my fault. They just missed out on preparing for their examinations, which didn't help, of course.

Look, more Spitfires. This was the RAF base at Northolt.

London was defended from here. Almost all the pilots were Poles. They were put on a regular training schedule, as if they were novices. During one of the sessions they caught sight of incoming German bombers and the squadron leader in charge of their training ordered the pilots to return to base. But they ignored him and began to communicate excitedly with each other in Polish. Then they carried out all sorts of complex manoeuvres and shot the German planes down. It turned out that they were just too polite to tell their British hosts that they didn't need training at all. They shot down more planes on average than English pilots.'

Do you count birds in the other direction, too?

'No, never. I keep an eye on the kites because they are so beautiful, but I know I will feel all right at Pelican House. Even or odd, it's all the same there.'

Can you cope with the computer at the TLS?

'No, I make changes to the copy by hand, then someone types them in. Belinda had this idea that when she retired, she would travel to Witney on her bus pass and take a computer course there. I was supposed to go with her.'

That sounds good.

'On the contrary. Wait till you've heard the name of the group that we were to join: The Silver Surfers!'

He laughs so hard that I fear for our safety, then he pulls up a little way from the road for a pee.

'I'm told this is a spot where men pick up other men. We'd better keep an eye on one another.'

Not long afterwards, when he is back behind the wheel, he asks, 'What are we drinking this evening? Old Tripp or wine?'

You choose. I noticed that Belinda didn't drink much at all yesterday.

'She's being careful. A few years ago she would get absolutely blotto just about every evening. She is wonderful when she's sloshed: she has the time of her life, then she falls asleep. I'm not so pleasant when I'm drunk; I can get into horrible rages.

When we were students – and for many years afterwards – we didn't drink at all, partly because we didn't have any money. But we gradually upped our alcohol consumption until we were each getting through two bottles of wine an evening – sometimes more. One day I read an item in *The Guardian* that classified alcoholics in nine different categories. The category that appeared to fit us was called "re-bonding" and involved husbands and wives coming home from work and drinking together to eliminate the tension of the day. It was on a higher plane than simply drinking until you keeled over. I believe that thirty-six units a week was considered pretty disastrous, and we were racking that up in a few days. Since then we have tried to cut down our intake somewhat.'

In the end we opt for a pint of Old Tripp each.

'Our journey is over. We have reached paradise. Let's ring Emile.'

He tells the publisher, truthfully, that we are exhausted. He also tells him, untruthfully, that Belinda and I winked at one another when he said that his mother always wanted to be the centre of attention. He concludes, 'Rudi talks to people and people answer – how unusual.'

He embroiders on this theme after the telephone call is over.

'When I'm abroad I talk to people, too, but in my own country I'm immediately relegated to a certain class. I sound posh, and people who are less posh automatically distrust me. You don't have that problem, because people can hear that you're a foreigner. You fall outside British categories: people are pleased that a foreigner is asking their opinion.'

He orders steak and mushroom pie, and compliments the waiter on the Old Tripp. 'Not that I've got any taste buds left to speak of, but this is really very good.

It was only recently that I appreciated why people like Bill Bryson's books so much. He goes to places that anyone can visit and writes amusingly about them. I like his style: he describes how he arrives at a hotel, how he goes out and how wonderful it is to sit and drink a pint somewhere – and I think, yes indeed, how true. That's the other great thing about it: it's so ordinary, but so true. Perhaps we should put photos of pubs in this book. Or of the B & B where we couldn't open the windows because we would endanger the ponies.'

We relocate to Pelican House. Earlier that day, before we had even got to London, I had asked whether I would be permitted to see his fetish room.

'For three seconds,' he had said. 'Perhaps.'

Meanwhile, befuddled by Old Tripp, this has slipped to the back of my mind, but Redmond can think of nothing else.

'It's like this,' he says, as we sit down with a glass of white wine. 'You're not allowed to talk to anybody about it. And you have to be very drunk beforehand. Drink. Drink more. Three seconds.'

After I see it, will I have to die?

'It's a real fetish room. Like the huts in the Congo, a little way off from the main dwelling. Marcellin said, "Don't take any photos, because I won't be able to protect you. People won't want to let you leave: they'll feel that they have to kill you."'

So you didn't?

'God, no.'

Since when have you had such a room?

'Since Douglas burned himself to death in the early seventies. In a way, it made him live on. I think of him constantly; he has become part of me. He was already a great artist, but his work was so intense that he could never have lived for very long.'

Did you always know that he was special?

'Yes.'

Did the reverse apply?

'I don't know. He never said much. We used to sit next to each other during Jack Halliday's biology lesson. We had to draw dissections and his drawings were masterly; full of emotion. He was a natural talent. People praised the strength of his line and all that kind of thing.'

Is his work still for sale?

'I've got nearly all of it. Does your back hurt?'

I can't feel anything.

'You're sitting as if you've got a sore back.'

He tries to get me to sit on a wobbly cushion. I stay where I am, possibly because the alcohol is by now acting as a general anaesthetic.

Redmond talks about a pony he brought back from Scotland for Puffin. 'Fifty pounds for the pony, four hundred pounds for transport.' It got to the point where the pony would roam about the house. 'That seemed perfectly natural.' But the pony did not stick to the rules. On reflection, there were no rules for a pony in the sitting room. The animal didn't feel at home surrounded by books. In the end it had to move.

Redmond fetches his thesis and then returns to the subject of the possible move.

'Maybe I've still got ten years of active life ahead of me. I haven't enough time for such a move. Just tell me that. Tell me it's impossible.'

It sounds as if you have serious doubts.

'I know I shouldn't, but I do. This has been a place of immense night-time effort for me. A place of sacrifice. Mainly

Pelican House, interior.

sacrifice of the family, incidentally. But at the same time I remember periods when I would go upstairs excitedly, when writing was going well, and I could hear the voices of my characters talking in my head. At moments like that I am weightless; I don't exist as a body, I only live in my mind, I am entirely with my characters. There is no greater happiness than that in the entire world. And I can attain it. At three o'clock I go to bed feeling somewhat guilty. In the mornings I re-read what I've produced, and I'm amazed. Did I write that? Each time I expect it to be rubbish. I think that with every book. Then I have to wait once more until nine in the evening. That's when I feel safe: no one will interrupt me. You must know that feeling too. You're not yet quite at your desk. You have left yourself behind. You are en route somewhere, on a journey, and in your imagination you experience it more intensely than when you were really there. If someone opens the door or asks a question at a moment like that, it's like being shot through the head. Awful. I get palpitations, feel as if I was dying. From nine until three in the morning I need to be left in peace. I work by artificial light. Not those ecologically sound light bulbs, but really good light. And the books come to life, they talk to me, I can think of nothing else except, occasionally, good God, how wonderful! When I think of someone like Wallace at moments like that, I feel excited, rather than dwelling on the fact that the poor sod is dead.

In daylight, books don't talk. There's just something preventing them. At night it is as if they come off the shelves and speak to you directly. They show every writer at his or her peak. That is my absurd idea of heaven. Tolstoy and Dickens come back to life. But as I'm experiencing happiness as a writer, I am leaving my family in the lurch.'

The family is asleep. And you're there during the day, aren't you?

'Not really then, either. Because I don't start on the stroke of nine o'clock. I first need to go through some tedious preliminaries. Reading, looking things up. As of three in the afternoon I have to start charging myself. Then I can hardly wait until it is dark.

As Martin Amis says, it's bad being a writer, because you're never entirely there for your family. You are always thinking of something else. But the same is probably true of bankers and politicians. Why should writers be more monstrous than other people?'

And these surroundings are essential?

'I've tried working in hotel rooms, but things don't come to life in an environment like that. It's all just chaos and white walls. In places like that I am only half a person. Here I am whole. Are you sure your back isn't hurting? I haven't forgotten about the fetish room. You must drink some more; you mustn't be sober.'

As if you could call me sober.

Redmond disappears for a moment, then comes back with books and an old pair of binoculars.

In one of the books that he hands me, I read 'Man was created by the Holy Trinity on 23 October 4004 BC, at nine in the morning.'

It is lucky that God didn't have the same working hours as you, I say.

Our conversation, recorded on tape, has now largely been freed from the logic of question and answer.

Redmond muses at random on a range of issues. 'I admire ambitious people. As I so often tell Bertie.' The cat disappears from his field of vision and he turns to another subject.

'Why are Russian writers so good? Because they write about families. Dickens writes about characters. Russians write about families and generations.'

His attention switches to the objects he has just fetched.

'Do you see these binoculars? They belonged to Thomas Alfred Coward, a great ornithologist who published the first popular bird book in this country, in three volumes. It was this book that my father gave me before I went to primary school. Even at that age I had the impression that he was trying to expiate his feelings of guilt.'

He has written his name in each volume. Redmond Douglas O'Hanlon. Two pounds ten shillings.

How did those binoculars come into your possession?

'My grandfather was an amateur geologist who used to go on field trips with Coward. They were good friends and when Coward died, he left his first editions and custom-built binoculars to my grandfather, who later gave them to my father. When I was nearly seven, my father gave them to me. And these are Morris's books, that I bought in Beach's Bookshop in Salisbury.

Drink. Drink more.

The idea of a fetish room is that you keep objects in it that have the basic power to excite you. In the way that sex excites you. Things from your past. Things that make you sweat. If they provoke that kind of response, you know you are getting near your subconscious. I can spend as much as a year repositioning objects, changing configurations again and again. I become desperate, because I don't seem to be getting anywhere. Then, suddenly, bang, it works. It's a kind of force field, generating enormous power. All writers need something. A room, or something in their head. This works for me. Or rather, it used to work. Now it doesn't any more, although it might recover its power one day. Everything is there. Galen Strawson once asked me, "Redso, do you ever add things to your fetish room?" The answer was no. I haven't added anything since a year before *Into* the Heart of Borneo. He really wants me to write.'

Would it help to add something?

'Yes. Could I have your feet? I need more feet. Feet are powerful. It's not something people talk about very much; perhaps we are ashamed of it.'

How often do you enter the fetish room?

'Sometimes I don't go there for ages, but when I'm writing I go every day, for about a quarter of an hour, to prepare. From that moment, no one is allowed to disturb me. When I'm there I go back to my childhood. Everything that was important for me is in that room. I think you could compare it to prehistoric caves with wall paintings. They were places for hunters; women were taboo. The caves were a reminder of the object of the hunt, but I think they were more important as a place where the men could empty their minds. It allowed them to stop agonising about whether their Homo sapiens bride was also doing it with the one-legged man who made arrowheads. I think that this has the same function.'

How does it work, precisely?

'That's the thing: it can't be described in words. I haven't got an explanation for it. It makes me sweat. It appeals to a deeper, more primitive part of my brain. It's a bit like what happens when I spend a week immersed in photography and suddenly lose the ability to speak. My brain has switched into some kind of visual mode, which makes the words seem absurd. I think this is comparable.

As recently as a few months ago, when I had decided to stop writing, I took Belinda and the children separately to see the fetish room. Five seconds each, to counter the rumour that I had hidden bodies there – because my children occasionally seemed to view me as some kind of Bluebeard.'

How did they react?

'They were appreciative. They saw my egg collection, including that one eggshell that fell at my four-year-old feet, as well as those other things that were important in my youth. They could see there was no mystery attached to it. Yet at the same time they never wanted to go there again.'

Belinda had already seen Douglas's foot, surely?

'She had picked it up herself. She was very fond of Douglas, but she felt that he sucked me into his deeply depressed universe. He would come to you in despair and you yourself would shrink under the weight of the mental burden that he carried.'

He shows me the fetish from the Congo, a child's or monkey's finger in a little pouch.

'Reason is all important to me. I am a convinced atheist.

The headmaster in Swanage loved birds. He told me that he did not think that ornithology could be a profession. The best way to go in for birdwatching, he said, was still to become a vicar. "And make sure that you get a parish on the coast," he went on, "because that's where you find the most interesting birds." He was right about that, and although he beat me, he did lend me his copies of a periodical called British Birds. Come to think of it, he gave them to me. When it came to birds, we were of the same mind. At that age I was absolutely convinced that I would become a vicar and have a big house, though I never pictured a woman coming to share it with me. That would have got in the way of the birds.'

Why birds, anyway, not mammals? Or plants?

'There weren't enough mammals to make it interesting and plants were too girly. I associated birds with freedom while I was a miserable prisoner at school. Unlike me, they had the power to come and go as they pleased, to fly away over the school walls. I have extraordinarily vivid memories of birds.

The nest of a goldfinch in the vicarage garden. By contrast with books, birds were very real. Messy, sometimes rain-soaked, with tousled plumage.'

He disappears again. When he returns, he is concealing something behind his back. He brings out his arm to reveal a jar, while at the same time humming the opening theme of Beethoven's Fifth Symphony.

'This is Douglas's foot.'

I am shocked, but on closer inspection I cannot see much more than a few little strips of dried flesh.

'For a long time I asked myself the classic questions: why him and not me, why not some untalented contemporary? I still dream of him regularly. In the dreams he is alive but no longer wants to see me. He has gone to live somewhere very far away. When I wake up I have to remind myself that he killed himself, not because he no longer wanted to see me, but for other reasons. I was not the centre of his universe; he had other interests and problems. Of course, he had never said that he was going to commit suicide. The letters only arrived after his death. He told me where I should look for him. He gave me all his work, his diaries. That would have made me love him, if I hadn't done so already. He enabled me to become a writer, by becoming part of me. I had to live for him as well. He only lived to be twenty-four.'

You were twenty-four as well, at the time.

'"I should have died, too", as I once wrote in a notebook. Had it not been for Belinda, that might have come true.

And now,' he says ceremoniously, 'this is only because I really like you ... and you must tell no one. Not even Emile. Unless it's in the book.'

He leads me outside. 'Follow me. Take a step to the right and then look to your left. All Douglas's work is here.'

He switches on the light. 'I'm starting to count now.'

A few seconds later the light goes out again.

I look left and right with such haste that I don't actually take anything in. I can see nothing bizarre or alarming, nothing obviously aesthetic. If anything, I see chaos. Then I see darkness, because the light has gone out. That is also my immediate memory of the room. Darkness. When I recall him counting it is with the light out. I feel exhausted and empty. A little dizzy.

'Are you okay? It's after midnight. Let's have one more drink and then go to bed.'

POSTSCRIPT

At secondary school, in one of our first history or geography lessons, my teacher explained the difference between extensive and intensive farming. I instantly realised that extensive farming was for me. At least, more so than intensive farming.

The ten days with Redmond were phenomenally intensive. In the night after the final evening, that intensity finally took its toll and I fell ill. My back went stiff. The pain that Redmond had been observing all evening, but that I had not yet felt, burst forth. I felt sick. I clung to and hung over the repaired toilet.

Five items on our list remained to be dealt with before I took the train to London. They included visiting Annabelinda and buying socks.

'You know what a Freudian would say,' Redmond commented half-jokingly. 'You are sick of me. And this project has broken your back.'

Even then I didn't think that he was right.

Redmond was solicitude itself. He drove me to a chemist

and recommended a certain type of painkiller (of purely theoretical benefit in my nauseated state, because you weren't supposed to take them on an empty stomach). He reduced our list to a single item: a lift to Oxford station. Indeed, he even wanted to scrap that. 'Shall I drive you to St Pancras?'

I staggered onto the train to London, weighed down by Redmond's parting gift of books. My malaise continued throughout the journey on Eurostar. By the time I got to Brussels I could eat enough to be able to take a painkiller. The nausea and backache soon cleared up, but I felt off colour for weeks, unable to shake off a kind of general hangover. I had drunk more on this trip than I would normally consume in an entire year. More, indeed, than in any other period of my life. Yet less than Redmond.

In the beginning I had only taped formal interviews, but as the trip advanced, I began to record virtually all our conversations. I had sixty hours of tape to listen to. For months I lived with Redmond's voice in my head. This peculiar form of possession was a strangely pleasant experience. I had been impressed at the time by his vast stock of anecdotes and the precision with which he told them, but listening to them again I was even more amazed.

This is not a biography. I have made no attempt at all to research other sources. I have, however, tried to avoid errors of fact. During my attempts to weed out inaccuracies I had written to Marlborough College, to be told that there is no official record of Redmond being expelled from school. According to the honorary archivist, Terry Rogers, that does not mean it did not happen. Whether or not sanctions were officially registered depended on the individual housemaster. The fact that Redmond was allowed to stay on a little longer because he was playing the lead in Hamlet was considered 'plausible'.

Marlborough College does incidentally, have all of Redmond's books in the library.

The second clarification concerns the story Redmond's mother used to tell with such relish, about the king who was murdered in Corfe Castle with a poker in the anus. It turns out that she was mixing up her Edwards. King Edward II, who was murdered with the famous poker in 1327, died at Berkeley Castle. The king who was killed at Corfe Castle was an earlier monarch, Edward the Martyr, who was stabbed to death in 978, possibly by order of his stepmother.

Thirdly, the planned journey to Spitsbergen has been cancelled. Redmond, who was not brimming with enthusiasm in the first place, was told by the Norwegian authorities that he would have to share a room with three students during a stay of several months. 'And that,' he tells me, through the hated telephone, 'was a bridge too far for me. I thought, I can't do this to myself. Whereupon my son Galen said, "You can't do it to those students".'

Fourthly, Redmond's father died towards the end of last year, at the age of ninety-seven. 'Four days before he died, my brother and I were warned that his condition was deteriorating and we went to visit him. He said nothing. As far as we could see, he was not in any pain. Then came a moment when I saw him very slowly raise his gnarled old hand. I thought, he is going to make the sign of the cross over us one last time. His hand just kept going up. Turned out he was trying to pick his nose.'

And there it was again, that hint of plaintiveness, as Redmond's guffaw rang out far across the Channel.